Successful Mission Teams

A Guide for Volunteers

Martha VanCise

New Hope
Birmingham, Alabama

New Hope
P. O. Box 12065
Birmingham, Alabama 35202-2065

Dewey Decimal Classification: 266.02
Subject Headings: MISSIONS
                       MISSIONS, VOLUNTEER—HANDBOOKS, MANUALS, ETC.
                       TRAVEL—HANDBOOKS, MANUALS, ETC.
                       MISSION ACTION

Illustration by Tim Towns

ISBN: 1-56309-169-0
N964131•0696•5M1

For Dave and Meribeth

Contents

vision alive—Effective linking—How you can help on the field—
Writing to missionaries—How to host a missionary family

Part Six: Disaster Assistance

*Work through an organization—Camping and cooking—Emergency food
list—Please, feed the animals—Don't plan on shopping—Clothing—Other
essentials—Garage sale items—Food donations—Tools—Tarps and plastic
covering—Miscellaneous—Identify yourself—Fifty-mile rendezvous—Stop!
before dark—Safety tips—Secure generators—Job description—Working
with disaster victims—In shock—Last days—It could be me—Witnessing to
disaster victims—Rooftop evangelism*

Before you go—On the mission tour—When you return home

Acknowledgments

I am grateful to the following friends who have contributed their collective knowledge of foreign missions: Don and Evelyn Adams, Eddy Cline, Wanda Dieudonne, Bryan Klassen, Raymond Phillips, Ron and Velma Vasselin, Roger and Lois Wood, and M. L. "Swanee" Schwanz.

Since my experience was in foreign missions, I am deeply indebted to the following people who contributed their ideas and observations about home missions: Larry Lansberry, M. P. "Buddy" and Sarah Taylor, Beth Montaño (Inner City), Dick and Vada Yoder (Inner City), Roger Harrington (Disaster), and Dean Johnson (Disaster).

Thanks to Jeanne Morgan, who kept praying.

A special thanks to my daughter, Meribeth, who both endured and supported my writing.

A very special thanks to my husband, Dave, who encouraged me to write this guidebook, and who also contributed to the manuscript. Several ideas contained in these pages came from briefing material which he developed as we worked with volunteers.

Introduction

My first encounter with mission volunteers occurred in Guatemala. Following the earthquake of 1976, my husband, Dave, and I directed a ten-month reconstruction project for the Salvation Army. Volunteers came from England, North America, and South America. They came through various relief organizations and from several religious persuasions. Many were devout believers in Christ; a few were agnostics or atheists.

After the project ended and I had time to evaluate the experience, I realized that some non-Christians, who fell into the category of "world travelers," performed better as volunteers than some of the Christians. Their ability to communicate cross-culturally surpassed mine, even though I was a committed Christian, had a Bible college education, and had some mission experience. I envied the relaxed way in which some of these "world travelers" handled the hardships of living in a semiprimitive camp and the way in which they communicated on a personal level with the Guatemalans.

The volunteers who had *both* experience as world travelers and who were committed to Christ, stood out as examples of the ultimate volunteer. As I reviewed the experience, I thought, *I'd like to work with volunteers again sometime. Next time, though, I think I can do it better.*

"Next time" came in the early 1980s, when Dave and I were asked to serve as missionaries in Haiti. As field directors of an interdenominational mission support organization, we directed volunteer teams full time. At that time, volunteer projects were just beginning to boom and very little material existed for orientation. Using our experience in Guatemala, my husband developed an orientation and debriefing program for our teams.

As we worked with members of almost every evangelical mission organization and denomination, and also with some nonevangelicals, I asked the missionaries, "How can we improve the performance of volunteers? What are you looking for in volunteers?" At first the missionaries murmured words of appreciation for the volunteers and brushed the questions aside. In time, though, they realized we were serious about improving the performance of mission teams and they began to tell us of problems volunteers had created. They were quick, also to tell of the ways volunteers had helped the cause of missions.

After returning to the States in 1989, we continued to direct some volunteer teams, and I continued updating our orientation material by means of travel tips from newspapers, magazines, and mission publications. Through correspondence and by direct contact, I kept asking missionaries who worked with volunteers, "Tell me about the best team you ever hosted. What made those volunteers exceptional? Tell me about the worst team? What did they do that volunteers should avoid?"

Out of the accumulated material and personal experience, I came to the same conclusions that most missionaries and leaders of volunteers have supported: successful volunteers exhibit attitudes of flexibility, openness, and servanthood.

Additionally, I discovered that volunteers with international travel experience and exposure to other cultures usually had an edge over other volunteers. Not only were they more comfortable with the vagaries of international travel and survival, but they seemed to hold no preconceived ideas into which they had to fit other volunteers, missionaries, or nationals. In foreign cultures, they stepped into the moment and enjoyed it for what it was. They were able to learn and receive from teammates and from the culture because they didn't feel pressured to fit into a mold themselves or force others into a mold. They focused on the culture and the people around them rather than on themselves. Instead of trying to leave their individualized stamps of self-sacrifice and spirituality on the culture and the people, they served as simple conduits through which the Spirit of God flowed to teammates, missionaries, and volunteers. The result was a relaxed, powerful witness.

The majority of foreign mission volunteers are as one missionary said, "The most loving, and giving members of the congregation." They are not usually, however, world travelers. For many, the mission experience is their first encounter with a different language and culture.

No matter how spiritual people are, if they are wondering how they will handle the next surprise, or if they are uneasy about committing cultural blunders, their minds will not be on ministry but on themselves. To focus on ministry, the volunteer must feel comfortable with international travel and cross-cultural relationships.

In deciding what to include in a guidebook for volunteers, I decided to make it a common sense, practical guide that would enable first-time travelers to feel like world travelers. The book is written in both a "showing," and "telling" manner. Anecdotes "show" the right and wrong ways to be a world traveler, and to model the necessary, volunteer qualities of flexibility, openness, and servanthood.

Concrete tips, action steps, cautions, and explanations of mission policies "tell" the volunteer how to put knowledge into action on the mission field and in the home church.

Today, many excellent volunteer training programs exist. They emphasize mental, emotional, and spiritual preparation for cross-cultural work. This book is not meant to take the place of any of these training programs, but rather it is a reference book to supplement existing programs. If you are serious about volunteer service, take advantage of every means of preparation that is available to you. If your church or the tour organization sponsors an orientation or training program, **be sure to attend all sessions,** even if you are a veteran volunteer.

In some areas, and in some churches, there are no training programs. I believe the information in this book will enable any committed Christian volunteer of average health, and emotional stability, to travel to a mission project, to have a productive volunteer experience, and to return home safely.

You can always go with more information than this guidebook provides, but don't leave home with less information.

As you read this volume, read it with pen in hand. Mark it. Refer to it as you prepare, travel, and return. Review it before taking additional tours.

Be prepared! Have a great mission experience!

Martha Van Lise

PART ONE

Before You Say Yes

CHAPTER 1

Commit Yourself to Preparation

Soap Operas and Puppy Love

Ron, a rotund, good-natured pastor from Indiana was about to realize his greatest dream—preaching on the mission field.

In a poor section which had no electricity, he chose as a
subject the "Soap Opera Lives of Joseph." The bilingual pastor
struggled with translation, then finally began preaching his own
message on Joseph. On the way home, Ron said, "It sounded to
me like the pastor said more than I did." My husband, Dave,
explained that people in many cultures, and especially those living in areas without TV have no concept of soap operas. We
encouraged Ron to think through the relevancy of his sermon
topics. "Look around," we advised. "Use images that these people
see every day."

The next night, he began his message by saying, "Puppy love

is real to the puppy." The national pastor shrugged and said to my husband, "I don't understand. What is the 'love of the puppy'?"

"Mission teams started a revival in my church that hasn't stopped," a pastor said. "When a group of my church leaders visited the mission field, they came home excited and their enthusiasm ignited our church. Mission giving has doubled. Each year, more teams go and more members come home eager to get involved in *all* the ministries of the church. Sending people to other countries is the best thing that ever happened to our church."

"Teenagers!" one missionary said, "Never send me a group of teenagers again. All they wanted to do was ride our motorcycles and go to the beach. They didn't work and when evening came they were too tired to participate in church services. Afterward, though, they could play loud music and roughhouse until 2:00 A.M. Next time, send them to church camp."

"Teens! What an encouragement," a national leader said. "Their luggage didn't arrive on time, but they never complained. They mixed concrete all day to build a clinic and spent the evenings getting acquainted with the young people in town. Send more."

When asked about his upcoming trip to Taiwan, Harry said, "I'm a little scared about going. I don't know what to expect." Another person on the 16-member team said, "I have no idea how to pack, all I know is that the weather will be hot." A pastor on the team said, "I'm not excited about going. It's going to be a whirlwind tour with no quiet time. Furthermore, we're at a crucial point in the building program of the church and I need to stay home."

"Popcorn! Popcorn and gravy! That's all they fed my people," one irate pastor exploded. "Don't talk to me about any more mission teams!"

A Dream Come True or a Nightmare?

For volunteers, the mission venture may be a life-renewing experience or a chaotic nightmare. Volunteers may supply funds to finish projects that would take the missionary and national workers ten years to complete. Or these volunteers, full of enthusiasm and ignorance, may also create problems which will take mission leaders ten years to resolve. What makes the difference between a "good" and a "bad" experience?

The key to a good experience for the volunteer and productive ministry on the field is **advance preparation.**

Sensory Overload

Sensory overload, especially the first day upon arrival in a foreign country, limits the amount of new information you can handle. In the back of your mind, anxieties linger over leaving home, family, and work. The novelty and chaos of the strange culture overwhelms. Language, traffic, smells, sounds, and masses of people assault the senses. Add to this sensory overload a day of travel (perhaps a first flying experience), meeting new team members, and the tension of protecting yourself and your possessions in strange surroundings. By evening, you will start shutting down mental input in order to cope with the enormous load you've received in a few hours. In the preliminary briefing session on the field, you may comprehend little more than "don't drink the water" and "be sure to put away valuables." Because of sensory overload on the field, **advance preparation is essential.**

Responsible Choices

Some volunteers will insist that they do not need instruction. Free-spirit types can grab a knapsack and wing it. They have a great time and come home with harrowing tales. Their accounts of "suffering for Jesus" make listeners shudder, develop chill bumps, and grow misty-eyed. These team members have exciting adventures, but they often leave behind a tangle of unnecessary chaos and discourage the timid from volunteering. If you plan to serve as a volunteer on a mission team, you have a responsibility to teammates, missionaries, nationals, and your home church to prepare for the tour. Preparation will not only ensure that you are an asset to the mission team, but it will make your trip more enjoyable and relaxing.

Check your calendar, talk with your family, and make sure that it's a sensible time to take a mission trip. Unlike overseas tours, home mission trips are usually within a one-day drive from home.

If an emergency arises, you can be home in a few hours and at no great expense.

Benefits of Advance Preparation

- Alleviates many fears and apprehensions.
- Eliminates a lot of unnecessary "suffering for the Lord."
- Enables the team member to concentrate on the new culture and ministry instead of concentrating on survival.
- Unifies a team and increases efficiency.
- Enables team members to gather concrete information to communicate to the home church.
- Lightens missionary and national leader workloads.
- Helps team members avoid many problems and misunderstandings.
- Helps team members forge strong links between the home church and missionary and national leaders.

CHAPTER 2

Conduct a Self-Evaluation Test

Everyone Should Go!!

No matter what team promoters may tell you, mission tours are not for everyone. A few years ago, my husband and I took relatives to Disney World. After a lengthy wait, we got on a log-flume ride. At the last minute, my brother-in-law who had been behind us disappeared. We found him waiting for us at the other end of the ride. "What happened to you?" we asked.

"I didn't go," he said. "I never do anything that makes me uncomfortable."

If you require comfort and predictability in your life, mission tours are not for you. Foreign and home mission tours will stretch and change you. If you enjoy adventure, surprises, making friends, and meeting challenges, pack your bags.

If this is your first flight or first overseas trip, expect a little apprehension. Anxiety concerning modes of travel and living conditions is normal. After years of accompanying work teams in an incredible variety of circumstances, I found myself anxious about a sailing trip to a remote Caribbean island. Fifteen of us would be crammed into an open, roughhewn sailboat for 4 to 14 hours—depending on the winds. My apprehension wasn't due to fear of high seas but the absence of toilet facilities.

To be honest, I was uncomfortable during part of the trip, but the discomfort was worth the once-in-a-lifetime chance to work on a primitive island. Those who insist on being comfortable all the time, miss many rewarding experiences.

If a foreign mission trip sounds like more than you can handle, consider involvement in home missions. No matter your talents, abilities, age, physical or mental limitations, you can find a place to serve on a home mission team. You don't even have to travel a long distance. If you take time to look, you'll probably find an opportunity for home mission work in your own community.

Some volunteers have found the home mission needs so vast, the work so challenging, and the experience so fulfilling that they have never looked beyond their homeland for mission work. Many of these dedicated volunteers devote extended periods of their lives to home missions. Other volunteers have found home missions to be an excellent training ground for foreign missions.

Wherever you serve, at home or abroad, *choose a volunteer service assignment that matches your abilities and gifts.* Perhaps your heart goes out to those who have no roof over their heads because of a hurricane, but if you hate being outside in the heat, a construction project in Florida in August isn't for you. Do be realistic about your physical, mental, and emotional strengths and limitations. Don't be afraid to stretch and try something new, but do be sensible about the type of mission trip you choose. You are entrusted with a spiritual ministry. You have a responsibility to prepare yourself by every means available.

Is It Time, Yet?
Be realistic about current events in your life. Is this the best time for you to take a mission trip? Some times are better than others. If you

need physical and emotional rest, pick a resort vacation. Choose the mission vacation another year. Choose another time if your wife is eight months pregnant; if you're behind in mortgage payments; if you're recovering from or anticipating major surgery; or if one of your parents is in the last stage of a terminal illness.

Be realistic. Can you afford to go? A mission tour may cramp your budget, but it should not add indebtedness. Guilt, concerning expenditure of money and home responsibilities, will dampen your enjoyment of a tour.

Can you get time off at work? One young man excitedly signed up for a tour saying, "If God wants me to go, He'll provide the time off." Six months later, after his plane ticket had been purchased and hotel room reserved, he asked for vacation time. The employer was short of help for those weeks and refused his request. The young man said, "I can't figure out why God put this on my heart but didn't work things out."

Seeing a need, and getting excited about it, doesn't mean that God will work miracles to put you on the mission field. Common sense should govern some choices. Ask for leave of absence before signing up, not two weeks before departure.

Don't let ordinary responsibilities keep you from going. Do, however, schedule your tour around major events on your personal calendar, otherwise your interest will be divided between home and the mission field.

One summer, my husband and I agreed to direct a mission team in Venezuela. To our surprise, our teenage daughter's softball team kept playing long after the regular season closed. The day that we boarded the plane with our mission team, our daughter left with her team to play in the Florida State Softball Finals. We found it difficult to concentrate on missions that week. Before signing up for a tour, check your schedule and check your children's schedules, especially if they are in athletics.

Be realistic in evaluating yourself and your circumstances. Some times are better than others to go on a mission tour. Be willing to be stretched, but also face the reality of closed doors.

Why Are You Going?

When teams first arrive on the field, missionaries often ask each team member, "Why did you come?"

One teenager answered, "My parents thought I needed to appreciate home more."

A pastor said, "My congregation thought I needed to visit the mission field."

Other answers have included:

"To fulfill a lifetime dream. I've always been interested in missions, and wanted a firsthand view of missions."

"I'm thinking of being a missionary."

"I love to travel and wanted to try a different vacation."

"I was here years before (on a cruise or when I was in military service), and I wanted to see the country again."

"When I heard the appeal for help, I had to come."

"My spouse (or friends) wanted me to come along."

These are a few of the many reasons team members give for taking a mission trip. Whatever your reasons for going, one reason must supersede all others—you are going to do a spiritual work. To do the spiritual work that mission tours require, you will need **flexibility, openness,** and **a spirit of servanthood.**

CHAPTER 3

Inquire About the Sponsor

All Mission Tours Are Not Created Equally

"Popcorn and gravy! That's all they fed my people. Popcorn and gravy!" the pastor exploded. "Do you think I'm going to let members of my congregation go to a mission field and be fed popcorn and gravy for a week? No, thanks. As far as I'm concerned, I'll never encourage my people to go on a mission team again."

"I can't imagine that kind of treatment," I said. "Was this your denomination?"

"No," he said and yanked open a file cabinet. He pulled out a folder and handed me a handwritten letter. Spelling and grammatical errors had been circled with red ink.

A little calmer, the pastor continued, "A member of the church met this pastor and was impressed by his work in the West Indies. We let the pastor speak at our church and share his concerns. He seemed desperate for help and the needs seemed so great that later, when he wrote specifically asking for our help, we quickly organized a work team and went down to build the school he needed. When we got there, he didn't have the foundation dug or any building materials on hand. The only food that he provided was popcorn and gravy! It was a waste of my members' vacation time and money. Don't talk to me about mission teams."

The handwritten letter, laced with praise phrases about the good-hearted people in the US and ending with a request to help children who lacked food, clothing, and education, was a duplicate of requests we had received weekly on the mission field.

I found it difficult to believe this midwestern church, that ministered to professionals, and had just launched a multimillion dollar building project, would give money and send church members to work with an uninvestigated organization. Emotion, however, over the plight of the poor and the need to "do something now" had overruled good common sense.

Watch Out for Mission Tour Scams

No matter how moving the appeal is for help, know the organization or group which is directing the tour. Mission tours are a vehicle for ministry; mission teams can also be a means of financial profit. Look for these three essentials in a tour sponsor or organization: financial accountability, accessibility, and a good track record. Beware of sound-alike-names in organizations and emotional pleas based on photos of starving children. Ask questions. How long has the organization been operating mission tours? Does it have a board? A budget? Can you reach the office by phone anytime you have questions? Is the office located in a specific place or do you correspond by post office box? Do you know anyone who has taken a mission trip with this organization? Did they have a good experience? You don't need to do a senatorial investigation, but do take a little time to make sure that you are dealing with a reputable organization.

You Can't Have It All

In photography, you seldom get exact lighting, fast shutter speed, and desired depth of field at the same time. You choose the most important effect and sacrifice other features to get the photo you want. In choosing a mission tour, there will be no perfect tour, so, keep in mind what is important to you. What do you hope to accomplish and learn on the tour? What are your physical and emotional limitations? Choose the type of tour that best fits your needs, and accept the less desirable aspects that may accompany it. Don't expect or demand what a tour does not offer. Be informed about what to reasonably expect.

Mission Organizations

Traveling under the auspices of a denomination or established mission organization has several advantages. Leaders will be aware of political, economical, and spiritual changes in the country and can give you a true picture of developing attitudes. Agents of established mission organizations will know where to obtain the best and nearest medical help. In the event of legal problems, or political upheaval, they will have preestablished contacts with your embassy.

Because established organizations usually cooperate with other mission agencies on the field, they can draw on a wide base of expertise and assistance to handle emergencies or unforeseen problems. Missionaries who live in the area can arrange economical and sanitary accommodations.

By working through established organizations, your time and money will go into projects which are the most productive in the long run. You can be assured that the project you sacrificed to complete will not be sold next year and the money pocketed by an individual.

On a well-organized project, materials will be delivered and preparations completed in advance of team's arrival. Someone—a missionary, or local businessman—will know where to purchase additional materials at the best prices. Translators will be with the team most of the time. The organization will supply major equipment such as cement mixers, generators, welders, and speaking systems. Mission tours operated by established denominations and mission organizations usually provide the best personal security and the best long-term return on your money and time. You will be limited, however, to that organization's concept of missions.

Even in home mission projects, work through proper channels for volunteer service. Loading your pickup truck with tools and appearing on someone's doorstep unannounced may give you a sense of really helping someone, but it's seldom the best use of your time and materials or the best way to meet a need.

Mission Team Specialists

When laypeople first began to visit the mission field in organized groups, missionaries supervised the teams. Although these teams completed construction projects, raised mission awareness back home, and generated needed funding, the missionaries soon discovered that preparation and supervision of teams disrupted their schedule. Conducting two to three teams a year seriously hindered the missionary's main ministry on the field. To handle this problem, many of the major mission organizations developed support branches to accommodate mission teams and appointed missionaries to work exclusively with teams. A few missions asked outside mission support organizations to supervise their teams.

Full-time missionaries who specialize in handling mission teams usually conduct excellent tours because they live in the foreign culture but maintain constant ties with the home culture. The regular missionary—who is immersed in the foreign culture—may possess more in-depth understanding of the country and customs but may not be able to communicate these concepts to team members fresh from the home culture. Because mission team specialists keep a foot in each culture, they are often able to communicate cross-cultural ideas to team members better than the field missionary.

If you are looking for in-depth and hands-on participation in missions, choose an established mission organization that provides a mission team specialist to direct the teams. Even the best preparations can fail, especially in developing nations, but career missionaries operating through established channels can cope with almost any emergency.

Travel Agencies

Many Christian-operated travel agencies have developed mission tour packages. These all-inclusive vacations provide Christian fellowship and tourist-type introductions to other cultures. They give the traveler a good first view of missions. Once you arrive in the foreign country, transportation is by chartered bus or van. Housing accommodations are in moderately-priced hotels or Christian-operated guest houses. A leader who has traveled in the country accompanies the team.

Expect to see the major attractions described in brochures and travel magazines. A tour usually includes sight-seeing jaunts, shopping, a visit to a "typical" home, and a church service. The mission phase of the tour will provide samples of mission work such as visits to orphanages, agricultural projects, and radio stations. A pastor may present needs and encourage you to financially support a school, feeding program, or a building project.

As far as advancing the missionary enterprise, these tours usually help generate funds for projects and increase mission awareness. They are excellent for the person who always wanted to see the mission field but is apprehensive about leaving home for a foreign land.

Reputable tour agencies will have contact people within the foreign country to assist you in case of a medical or diplomatic emergency. As with any travel plans, know your agency. Some offer excellent mission-centered tours; some are only packaged moneymaking schemes. Remember the best references come from someone you know who had a good experience.

In most cases, avoid work projects arranged by a mission travel agency. Travel agencies seldom provide the in-depth briefing required to work effectively with people of another culture, and they leave the logistics of operating a project in the hands of team members. Horror stories abound concerning teams that assumed too much from a tour agency. Some teams have been dropped off in remote areas without building materials, transportation, interpreters, bedding, or even adequate food and water.

Overall, travel agencies are an excellent choice for a broad first view of a country and mission opportunities but not a good choice for a work project.

Single Church Sponsors

Sometimes an independent church in North America will send evangelism and construction teams to establish a new mission work. If your goal is to help establish the work, then the mission tour will serve your purpose. Unless these teams are directed by a veteran missionary or a longtime resident of the country, however, your perceptions of the culture and global missions will be limited and biased. Again . . . the choice is yours. Choose the tour that you like, but accept the limitations of the tour you choose.

Freelancer (North American)

There are exceptions, but for the most part be wary of tours directed by a North American freelancer who has not lived in another culture. Also, be wary of a national leader who hosts a team of North Americans without having lived in their culture.

These tour leaders sincerely desire to promote missions, but lack understanding of other cultures and modern missions. Some North Americans see a need and rush home to recruit a mission team. Well-intentioned, but uninformed, they escort teams back to the mission field and supply them with a theme-park description based on anecdotes they have heard. Because these team leaders do not live in the country, they cannot separate fact from hearsay. Furthermore, they do not detect changes in attitudes, politics, and socioeconomic patterns. Although they may have accompanied teams every summer for ten years, they still do not really understand the culture. Because they see only surface problems, and haven't had time to delve into the underlying cause of problems, they encourage team members to leap in with adhesive bandage assistance.

Exceptions do exist. If you choose a tour directed by a North American freelancer, look for these qualifications in the leader:
• Extended periods of living in a foreign culture;
• Training and experience with established mission organizations;
• Acceptance on the mission field and in homeland churches as a knowledgeable director of teams;
• Continued affiliation and cooperation with established mission organizations.

If you find a freelancer with these qualifications, you can be reasonably assured of a good mission experience.

Freelancer (National Leader)

Problems with tours led by national leaders usually result from lack of understanding of North American culture, and the workload of caring for a team of 15 to 20 volunteers. If meals are eaten in restaurants and housing is in a motel, the workload is manageable. Caring for 15 North Americans in a remote area, however, is a logistical nightmare which only experienced leaders should attempt.

The pastor who served popcorn and gravy to team members probably thought he was prepared to handle a team. He needed a school and had asked the people in Ohio for help. He left the planning up to the Americans and did not realize that they would expect him to have building materials on the job site. On the other hand, the Americans probably did not realize that the pastor had no money with which to purchase materials.

As for the pastor's provision of food, in his culture people ate rice and beans every day. He probably heard that Americans love popcorn and pour gravy on everything, so he went to great effort to locate and purchase the expensive packaged food that he thought pleased Americans.

Exceptions do exist. Some national leaders conduct excellent tours. If you choose to go on a tour sponsored by a national leader, look for these qualifications:
• An extended period of residence in the United States or Canada;
• Experience with handling mission teams;
• Cooperation with, and recognition by, established churches and mission organizations on the field.

Even when dealing with reputable freelancers, keep in mind their limited access to equipment, supplies, and emergency assistance. In the event of a medical or political emergency, you may find yourself on your own.

In spite of the weaknesses of teams operated by free-lancers, they enjoy popularity for three reasons. First, they are led by personalities. A charismatic leader—possibly someone you have personally met—is easier to follow than an unknown mission representative who meets you at the airport. Second, these leaders often give the volunteers what they want—an emotional experience. Rather than presenting a balanced view of all mission work, they focus on hungry or diseased children. Last of all, the price is right. Trips organized by freelancers are tailored to fit the tight budget. Team members pay only the real cost of food and transportation plus a little to cover the leader's expenses. In some cases, team members who sign up ten members can travel free.

Mission organizations cannot compete with the prices of freelancers because of overhead costs such as vehicle and equipment maintenance, staff salaries, and insurance. To some people, cost is the most important factor in determining a mission tour. Remember, you run more risk of misusing your time and money the farther you get from organized missions. In missions, as in any other enterprise, quality has a price.

Mission teams, which are gaining the respect of the missionary community and are making viable contributions to global missions, are those that are directed by qualified leaders with cross-cultural training and experience.

CHAPTER 4

Decide on the Specifics

Traveling Companions

"I'm stuck here with a knee-jerk evangelist," the postcard read. A team member had placed it on my desk to be mailed. Anyone approaching the desk, including the evangelist, could have seen the comment. Later that day, a woman on the team said, "Several of us are meeting upstairs in a prayer circle. Would you like to join us? We are going to pray for Dan." I declined. The team, made up of people from several churches, had divided along theological lines. Dan was a young pastor who held liberal views.

Fellow team members will help shape your mission tour experience. Team makeup may consist of representatives of a single church or of several churches in a single denomination. On these teams, shared experiences, acquaintances, and beliefs help develop unity quickly. If this is your first mission trip and you haven't traveled much, you'll probably want to travel with friends.

Other tour groups are composed of members from several denominations and several geographic locations. Traveling with strangers from different backgrounds will broaden your perspective of missions, but it will also provide more possibilities for personal conflict. Traveling in harmony with teammates who may challenge, rather than agree with, your views will definitely require openness to learning and willingness to serve. If you are comfortable with international travel, love adventure, enjoy making new friends, and want to broaden your worldview, try a multibackground team.

I Wanna Go Home

Mission trips usually range from 4 days to 14 days. Ten days seem to be ideal. Every summer Cathryn spent two weeks helping in Vacation Bible Schools on a foreign mission field. One spring she wrote saying that she would like to participate in two teams: a music team and the Vacation Bible School team that followed. We replied, "Four weeks is a long time to be on teams. Are you sure that you want to stay this long?"

She insisted on staying four weeks, but halfway into the third week she began to withdraw from the culture. She complained of being tired and slept in at the guest house rather than going out with the team. Alone during most of the day, she began to miss home and her family. In the evening, she depressed other team members by complaining about the food and inconveniences in the country. She was experiencing culture shock.

If you choose to stay longer than two weeks, be aware that culture shock is progressive. Be prepared to deal with some anger, resentment, and depression as the novelty of the country wanes.

If you choose a home mission project, go with the intention of finishing the tour. In foreign service, distance, expense, and unfamiliarity with the culture force the volunteer to accept things as they are and endure until the tour ends. In the home culture, it's different. We either change situations that we don't like, or we walk away from them. Enduring what we consider as unnecessary discomfort is seldom on our agenda.

As one pastor said, "If volunteers don't like the job or

accommodations, they sometimes leave in a huff." Do go with the intention of making the most of the situation and "endure hardship . . . like a good soldier of Christ Jesus."

Is There Anything for Me to Do?

Opportunities to serve on the mission field are limitless (see suggestions that follow). Many mission trips involve renovation or new construction. No matter your age, your manual skills, or physical strength, these trips offer opportunities for everyone to participate.

Besides framing, roofing, block laying, troweling, running electrical wires, and plumbing, volunteers are needed to paint, pick up trash, sweep out the construction site, prepare meals, run errands, and carry cold drinks to workers who are too busy to stop. On one project, two 70-year-old women sanded, punched nails, and cleaned windows. An 80-year-old man swept out the building daily. One woman who was mentally impaired set the table for the team members each day and cleared up after them. Sometimes, just coming to support a mate, carry drinks, rub a sore back, and prepare a good meal will enable volunteers to accomplish a lot of work. Everyone loves to do a big job such as roofing or dry walling that can be photographed, but the little jobs that no one sees hold a big project together.

One Florida pastor who hosted several home mission teams said, "I wish volunteers realized that no one thing can be labeled unimportant, and no one thing is more important than another. No amount of time is too little. Everyone can participate."

Make adequate preparations for your work. This means taking construction tools that you will need, audiovisual equipment, children's ministry props and materials, etc. When one couple arrived at a rural church to do a Vacation Bible School, they found that the church had no materials. The husband was so upset he refused to help. It is better to be overprepared than underprepared.

Preparation sometimes involves getting permits or applying for licenses. If you are planning construction, medical assistance, canvassing, or public evangelism projects, make sure that the local congregation has obtained the necessary permits in advance.

When choosing a tour, decide if you want to use your expertise on the mission field or if you want a vacation from your regular work. In making a choice, take into consideration your health, professional experience, talents, physical strength, and likes or dislikes.

Volunteer mission opportunities can be divided into three basic categories: ministry among people with an average or above standard of living; ministry among the poor; and ministry among people in disaster situations.

Mission projects among people with an average or above standard of living may include children's ministries or outreach/evangelism programs, but most often, they are construction or renovation projects.

While *individual* volunteers minister in a variety of ways among the poor, *teams* of volunteers usually handle Vacation Bible Schools, medical clinics, and construction projects.

Unless you have personally witnessed or worked in a major disaster you cannot comprehend the resulting chaos. Life as we know it ceases. Safe water, food, electricity, and communications are nonexistent. Without shelter, people are vulnerable to the elements, additional injury, and crime. All that is familiar vanishes: landmarks, businesses, schools, churches, and homes. Many victims go into shock. Some never recover. The preparation involved with a disaster relief ministry is extensive; you will find an entire chapter dedicated to this type of mission work at the end of the book.

The opportunities for volunteers are endless. Check out the options before you make a decision.

Opportunities to Serve

Construction	Literature Distribution
Vacation Bible School	Youth Camps—Nationals
Evangelism	Youth Camps—Missionaries'
Music Evangelism	Kids
Medical	Pastoral Training Seminars for
Agricultural Assistance	Nationals
Craft Instruction	Family Seminars for Missionaries
Religious Surveys	

Physical Limitations

Do be realistic about your age and any physical disabilities. Don't let physical limitations keep you from going, but do choose a tour that you can handle. On one project, team members had to negotiate a steep slope to get to the work site. A college team came first, and one girl broke her leg in two places. When the second team arrived, the missionary in charge was appalled. One man was nearly 80 years old.

Asking ahead about transportation and accommodations is not a sign of wimpiness or unwillingness to "suffer for Jesus." If you have physical limitations, inquire about the climate, altitude (people with lung and heart problems have difficulty in high altitudes), job site, and type of work you'll be doing. You may want to ask about location of medical assistance. Facilities may be as near as the mission clinic or a day's mule ride away.

Blow-dryers and River Baths

In choosing a tour that suits you, take into consideration the accommodations. Tour accommodations fall into three basic categories: modern, semimodern, and primitive. Some tours may offer all three types of accommodations. Be realistic about what you can handle, but be willing to be stretched.

Modern—Usually a hotel or guest house, which will be comfortable but not luxurious. Indoor plumbing, possibly hot water. Electricity most of the time.

Semimodern—Dormitory accommodations in churches or in homes of missionaries or nationals. Share a bathroom with the team. Cold showers. Either no electricity or electricity limited to certain hours.

Primitive—Tents or sleeping arrangements in a church, school, or homes of nationals. Beds are usually cots or pieces of foam on the floor. No electricity or running water. Outhouse. Bathe in river or use camp shower.

The farther you get from the tourist areas, the more realistic your view of the country and its people will be. If you are athletic, enjoy camping, and don't mind bathing in rivers, go for the primitive camping. If you are healthy and fairly adventuresome, the semimodern tour is excellent for a first timer. If you have health problems, scream at the sight of bugs, or must have your blow-dryer, stick with the modern tour. Don't choose something you simply can't handle. Recognize your tolerance levels to inconvenience, but be willing to be stretched.

Four Basic Food Groups

Food will usually come from one of these four sources.

1. Team brings food and cooks it. Fresh fruits and vegetables are bought locally. Familiar food.
2. Missionary staff prepares meals. Team members bring in some food. Familiar food with a few local dishes.
3. Restaurant—Combination of national dishes and familiar foods with a foreign flavor.
4. National church—Members of national church prepare meals using local food. Food will be distinctively foreign and have little variety.

The tour that everyone else in your church or circle of friends takes may not be the one you will enjoy. Take a good look at what a mission tour offers before making a decision.

Be informed. Choose the tour that best fits your needs. Remember, you can't have it all. Compensate for the shortcomings of your tour and accept what cannot be changed. Don't expect what your tour does not offer. Focus on the positive aspects of your tour, and get ready for a memorable trip.

Session One

Individual or Group Assignments

Choose Your Tour Test

To help you choose the right mission tour, check the items below that are important to you.

1. Being with friends or people who share similar likes and views.
   ❑ YES   ❑ NO

2. Seeing major tourist attractions and going shopping.
   ❑ YES   ❑ NO

3. Participating in hands-on projects and interacting with the local people.
   ❑ YES   ❑ NO

4. Eating familiar foods.
   ❑ YES   ❑ NO

5. Comfortable accommodations.
   ❑ YES   ❑ NO

6. Physical exertion limited to moderate activity. No hard physical labor.
   ❑ YES   ❑ NO

7. Being able to reach medical help within an hour.
   ❑ YES   ❑ NO

8. Low price.
   ❑ YES   ❑ NO

9. Getting away from tourist areas. Seeing how local people really live.
   ❑ YES   ❑ NO

10. Participating in a project launched by my home church or a particular national leader.
    ❑ YES   ❑ NO

In choosing a tour, take into consideration the items you marked *yes*. You may, however, have to sacrifice one *yes* for another. For example: I would mark *yes* to items 3, 5, 6, and 9. I could sacrifice comfort (5) in order to get away from tourist areas (9). I could not, however, handle a 10-hour mountain hike to a remote location and sacrifice (6). **Know yourself. Know your tour.**

Questions to Ponder and Discuss

1. Why do I want to take a mission tour?
2. Do I sense God's leading in this direction? Are doors opening in this direction in the areas of: finances, work schedule, and/or family responsibilities?
3. Am I willing to be stretched physically? Mentally? Emotionally? Spiritually?
4. Am I willing to give up my individual rights for a couple of weeks in regard to comfort? Choice of food? Choice of companions? Am I willing to give up personal choices in order to be part of a team?

Assignment

Prayerfully consider which mission tour is right for you. After you have made your decision:

- Send in registration forms and fees.
- If you do not have a passport, get application forms from the post office. Have passport photos taken.

PART TWO

Early Preparation

CHAPTER 5

Paperwork

Go to Serve, Not Save

Seasoned travelers may pack and leave on a mission trip with 24 hours' notice, but most people need several weeks to prepare. Early preparation will not only eliminate many last-minute anxieties, but also spread out costs and give you time to make necessary purchases at discount prices. (Chapters 8 through 10 give packing and purchasing suggestions.)

While everyone is concerned about saving money, abandon the idea that you take a mission tour to save money. Many people readily spend "big bucks" on ski and dive trips but suddenly develop guilt feelings about spending money for a mission trip. Choose a mission tour to serve, not to save.

As soon as you make the decision to go, mail registration fees to the tour organization. In return you should receive information on the following:

• Documentation

- Immunizations
- Financial arrangements
- Description of climate, basic accommodations, and job or tour description
- Code of conduct and dress
- Baggage allowance
- Packing guidelines

Documentation: Always Travel with a Current Passport

Traveling without a passport is possible in some countries, but it is never convenient. Keep in mind that every individual passes through immigration alone. Since the US has no uniform documentation of drivers' licenses and birth certificates, foreign immigration agents who read little or no English may have difficulty picking out birth dates and registration numbers on your documents. Furthermore, married women usually have different surnames than the name on their birth certificates. Having a familiar US or Canadian passport, will prevent confusion when dealing with non-English speaking immigration officials.

A passport will also make reentry into the US easier. In many US international airports, US citizens with passports are waved through immigration with a quick glance at the open passport. US citizens without passports are directed to wait in line until their documents can be carefully checked.

People neglect getting passports for two reasons: cost and uncertainty about how to obtain one. A passport is a necessary expenditure. Remember that you are part of a team. When all members of a team have passports, everyone can move smoothly through immigration. Put out the extra effort and money to help the team operate efficiently.

The procedure for getting a passport is simple, but will take a little time. Passport agencies are located in courthouses and some post offices. If you are applying for a passport for the first time you will need to apply in person. Before going, call and ask when the passport window will be open. When you go, take with you:

1. **Proof of US citizenship.** This may be a certified birth record (with official seal and date of filing) or naturalization papers or old passport.
2. **Proof of identity.** This is a document with photo and signature such as a valid driver's license or military ID.
3. **Two photos.** These must be taken within the past six months and be full-face view, two-inches square with a plain white background. Do not wear head covering unless required by your religion. One-hour photo labs in shopping malls do passport photos.
4. **Payment.** Take a check, money order, or exact change for each application.
5. **Completed application form.** The form can be obtained from the post office.

If you are renewing a passport, you can get the form from the post office and renew by mail. Processing takes four to six weeks, depending on low or high travel season. Also, allow more time if you need to send for visas.

Visas

Check with the mission organization about visas. Some visas are purchased at the airport at departure time. Others must be obtained in advance. If you are traveling to more than one foreign country, be sure to have visas for each country.

Immunizations

Always have your tetanus shots up-to-date, even for home mission projects. (Booster shots are needed every ten years.) Other immunizations will vary with the country or situation. Changes in the way immunizations are administered occur constantly. Immunizations that require a series of shots today may require only a pill tomorrow. As soon as you know which immunizations you will need, call your doctor. The doctor can then schedule immunizations so that they are completed before your departure.

Doctors in your local church may provide free or low-cost immunizations, or your family physician may give you a discount if you explain the purpose of your trip. Local health care services will also provide some immunizations free. **If you are pregnant,** be sure to notify the doctor. Some immunizations should not be given if there is a possibility that you may be pregnant.

Financial Arrangements

The tour organization should clearly state what your tour fee includes. Look for information on: air transportation, visas, departure taxes, ground transportation, tips, food, lodging, sight-seeing, and entry to tourist attractions.

Job or Tour Description

You should receive basic information on climate of the country, location of the project, the type of tour or work you will do, and the type of accommodations to expect.

Code of Conduct and Dress

Denominations, countries, and communities within a country usually have basic behavior and dress codes. These restrictions may seem an imposition on your Christian liberties, but part of servanthood is the laying down of your "rights" to accomplish the goals of the Master. Check the organization's guidelines and take them seriously. As a rule, most mission organizations forbid the use of drugs, alcohol, tobacco, and profanity. Some forbid card games. Team guidelines usually include a statement on shorts, slacks, and sundresses for women and shorts for men. Often these restrictions are not based on religious beliefs, but rather cultural mores practiced by both Christians and non-Christians.

Baggage Allowance

The baggage allowance is usually more than adequate. Occasionally, however, you may fly on private mission planes. On them, you may be limited to one bag ranging in weight from 25 to 40 pounds.

Packing Guidelines

This information will list any special items related to your work (hammer, trowels, etc.) or personal items needed (mosquito netting, sunscreen, etc.).

CHAPTER 6

When I Was
a Missionary . . .

Glowing Missionaries

"When I was a missionary in Honduras . . ." The words were spoken by a young man barely out of his teens who attended a conversational Spanish class in a Florida community college. He glowed with enthusiasm and tried to interject gospel messages into his Spanish assignments. As a veteran missionary of four weeks, he had a lot to share with the class.

The instructor, who had lived many years in Ecuador and had married an upper-class Ecuadorian, politely smothered smirks and continued to devote one segment of each class to cultural studies. Gradually, the young man's comments ceased. Finally, near the end of the semester, he said, "I sure made a lot of mistakes. I'm surprised that people in Honduras put up with me. I wish that I had known some of these things ahead of time."

Vacationing Missionaries

One US businessman who was visiting a Caribbean country joined a work team. To the missionaries he confided, "I sure wouldn't want my friends to know that I was hanging out with missionaries." Within a few days, however, he began using the phrase "*we are missionaries,*" as a business password. He thought the title would get him faster service and cut red tape. Using his new title, he made friends at the US embassy and received an invitation to a monthly party held by the US Marines. At the party, a marine noticed his frequent trips to the rum punch and said, "I thought you were a missionary."

"Oh, I am," he replied, "but I'm on vacation from being a missionary."

Fantasy Missionaries

Some team promoters promise the opportunity to "be a missionary" for a couple weeks. The concept is similar to baseball fantasy camps, barefoot cruises, and dude ranches. For two weeks you can fulfill a lifetime dream.

People who attend a baseball camp may be photographed in uniform and play actual ball games with the stars, but they do not walk away from camp and call themselves major league baseball players. They understand that paying a fee and showing up on the field does not transform them into professional players. They understand that major league players achieve their status through years of sacrifice, family separation, physical pain, and work.

One of the most important steps to successful volunteer ministry is getting a clear picture of your role. You may participate in evangelism or construction alongside a missionary, and you may observe the inside logistics of mission work, but this involvement will not make you a missionary.

In global missions, the term *missionary* is an earned title that represents work, commitment, and sacrifice. Almost all career missionaries have received college degrees, trained in specialized fields, and served internships. Many have sold homes and given up lucrative incomes in order to serve on the mission field. They have spent months on speaking tours and months in language study. The term *missionary* is not an honorary degree to be handed out casually to mission team members. It is an earned title. The saying, "Everyone is either a missionary or a mission field," may be a catchy slogan to raise mission teams, but it is about as realistic as "everyone is either a doctor or a patient."

Home-Field Links

Although you may lack the preparation to serve as a missionary, *you can fill a gap in global missions that no one else can fill.* You can link your home church to the mission field. Just as volunteers cannot adequately function as missionaries, many missionaries have difficulty relating to their home culture when they return from the field.

Missionaries operate from a worldview and sometimes have trouble seeing from the limited viewpoint of those who have had little or no contact with other cultures. Their stories, although intriguing and exotic, sometimes seem far removed from everyday, North American life. Missionaries who have lived in underdeveloped countries for several years often suffer from reverse culture shock. They find it hard to relate to those in affluent cultures.

Furthermore, the North American demand for rapid visual and audio messages created by professional communicators often limits the missionary's effectiveness. Unless the missionary is a powerful and entertaining speaker, audiences quickly grow restless.

If the missionary addresses a sizeable congregation, personal contact will be limited to a greeting and handshake. Only a few people will bother to wait and inquire about topics of special interest.

Taking the "Foreign" Out of Foreign Missions

The home-field link takes the foreignness out of mission experiences. Team members relate stories from much the same perspective as listeners would experience the events firsthand. Volunteers also have more time to tell their story.

While tight travel schedules limit the missionary's time in home churches, lack of time seldom hinders the ministry of mission links. In casual conversation extending over months, team members can relate anecdotes from the mission field. In their one-on-one contacts with members of the congregation, they can answer questions or describe needs that would appeal to special interest groups. For example, one team member may explain to teachers the need for more desks in a Christian school. Another member may discuss with farmers the need for hybrid seeds in an agricultural co-op.

The missionary who speaks during one service may create a splash of mission interest, but home-field links can penetrate and permeate the entire church body with mission awareness.

Home-Field Links in Action

After serving three years in Haiti, my husband and I returned home for a speaking tour. In some churches, we met an attitude of "Prove to me that mission teams aren't boring—quickly!" After the service, a few people would show interest, but the majority of people would politely shake our hands and head for the door.

When we entered churches that had sent mission teams to work with us on the field, we found congregations anticipating our arrival. Through personal anecdotes, told over a period of several months, team members had linked us to congregations.

The volunteers' conversations with us on the field also enabled us to gear our presentations toward real interests in their home churches.

We did not enter those churches as strangers who needed to sell missions, but as friends of team members in the church. The people who attended these services listened attentively and took time after the service to talk with us.

Home-field links cannot take the place of missionaries on the field, but they can dramatically increase the missionary's effectiveness at home. Volunteers who go to the mission field to be a "missionary" will experience the satisfaction of limited accomplishment for two weeks. Volunteers who focus on linking the home church to the mission field will find unlimited opportunities to minister over several decades. Your role as a home-field link is vital to the future of missions. Don't take your responsibility lightly.

CHAPTER 7

Spiritual Preparation

Don't Leave Home Without It

The Caribbean mission tour wasn't exactly like home, but it offered the comforts of American-style food and hotel-type accommodations, including hot showers. One team member, however, complained constantly. He grumbled about the food, insisted on always having the front window seat in the van, and refused to do manual labor on the planned project. Although churches of his denomination were located several miles from the project, he demanded that the missionary show him the churches. Fellow team members were shocked at the man's selfish attitudes. He was a pastor.

On the mission field, you may be able to fake education, wealth, success, or expertise, but you won't be able to fake spiritual life. Under the pressures of little privacy, strange food, limited bathroom facilities, heat, insects, and crowded vehicles, your inner life will soon emerge. The mission field quickly separates those who speak of the fruit of the Spirit from those who possess the fruit. If you plan to serve the cause of global missions, **don't leave home without a vital, growing, spiritual life.**

Spiritual preparation cannot be left to the last minute. You can't pray on the way and suddenly become spiritually sensitive, patient, and servant-minded when you cross the county line, the city limit, the dateline, or the country border.

Oswald Chambers, author of *My Utmost for His Highest,* served God in Japan and Africa. He wrote, "If you have not been worshiping as occasion serves, when you get into [mission] work you will not only be useless yourself, but a tremendous hindrance to those who are associated with you."[1]

Start a Spiritual Fitness Program Today

If you have never taken development of your spiritual life seriously, start now. First make sure that you have a proper relationship with God. All of us sin and fall short of what God requires. Our sins separate us from God. The ultimate consequences of our sins will be judgment and death. Christ, though, took the penalty for our sins on Himself, when He died on the cross. He is the mediator between us and God. We can be reconciled to God by confessing our sins and accepting the gift of forgiveness and salvation which Christ has provided. If you are uncertain about your relationship to God, begin by confessing your sins and accepting the gift of salvation.

Through attending a local church, reading the Bible, and taking time to pray, you will gain new insights about God and His plan for your life. Applying the new knowledge to everyday situations at home, work, school, or church may often be difficult. Obedience, however, to God in the mundane events will prepare you to make right choices on the mission field.

In speaking of preparation for missionary work, Chambers also said, "The characteristics we manifest in our immediate surroundings are indications of what we will be like in other surroundings."[2] Only if you master the lessons of patience and servanthood at home, can you expect to manifest those attitudes on the mission field.

To further prepare yourself for spiritual service, read books on servanthood, discipleship, and mission-related topics. Biographies of missionaries are excellent choices.

If you can, pray with a teammate or a friend on a regular basis about the upcoming trip. Ask God to prepare your heart, the hearts of your teammates, and the people you will meet on the field. Pray also that God will direct you in the preparation of your personal testimony.

Tips for Spiritual Preparation

- Have a vital, growing, personal relationship with Christ.
- Practice spiritual disciplines: church attendance, Bible study, and prayer.
- Pray about going, the type of project, the time to go, and the location.
- Enlist prayer partners. The couple who worked in Phoenix said, "The prayers of our friends helped us avoid pitfalls that would have hindered our work."
- Look at everyday, ordinary experiences and problems as training for home missions.

I'll Just Open My Mouth and Trust God to Fill It

"Write out your message ahead of time," the missionary told the young pastor, who planned to deliver a short message through an interpreter.

"I've had a lot of preaching experience," he replied. "I don't really think it's necessary to write out my message."

Maybe it was the whine of mosquitoes or the hiss of the gas lantern that distracted the pastor. Whatever the reason, he lost his train of thought during the translation and became hopelessly confused. In tears, he asked the missionary to close the service. The young man walked out of the thatch-roofed church that night, vowing never to preach on the mission field again. The young man's failure could have been avoided. With proper, advance preparation, anyone can give a personal testimony through an interpreter.

Tips for Translatable Testimonies

1. Write out your testimony. No matter how comfortable you are with public speaking, you should write out your testimony. If you can deliver your testimony without referring to the notes, great! But if you get distracted by the translator or a commotion in the congregation, you'll wish you had notes to get back on track.

2. Keep your comments brief. Unless you are the primary speaker, a 3-minute testimony is adequate. With a translator, the message will take 5 minutes to deliver. If you are the main speaker, plan for 20 minutes or less. With the interpreter, this will run 30 to 40 minutes.

3. Open with a greeting in the people's language. Even if your accent is terrible, the people will appreciate your effort to communicate in their language.

4. Tell what Christ has done for you personally. How were you convinced of your need of a Savior? How has your life changed since Christ came in? How has Christ helped you recently? Quote Scripture references, if possible, but make sure they are appropriate. Don't just tack on a Bible verse. When speaking of the plan of salvation, make sure the steps are clear and easy to understand. Don't rely on an interpreter to clear up a muddy presentation. Some interpreters are not Christians.

5. Avoid going into detail about your sins in the past. Emphasize the redemptive work in your life.

6. Avoid slang or idioms. Think about what you are saying. What do your words mean, literally? How would "a ball park figure," or "his face fell," or some current slang term translate?

7. Avoid long sentences.

8. Avoid Christian clichés such as "soul-saving station."

9. Avoid references to small geographical areas in the US or Canada. Your audience's knowledge of US geography will

probably be limited to New York City, Miami, or Los Angeles. Rather than saying you came from Illinois, Colorado, or North Carolina, tell them you grew up in the flatlands, in the mountains, or along the sea.

10. Avoid stressing your material success. Some in the congregation may put in 14 hours of hard, manual labor each day and still not have a change of shoes. In other countries, dreams plus hard work don't always equal material success.

11. Avoid speaking of the sacrifice you made to get there.

12. Avoid using acronyms, acrostics, alliteration, jokes, and poetry. They simply do not translate as you think. Don't quote from songs. In some languages the lyrics of familiar hymns have been rewritten to fit the music meter.

More Than Humanitarian Work

"Our home mission work in inner-city Phoenix prepared us for service in India," one couple said. "Without that preparation, we could have never handled the sights we saw in India. Working with the homeless in Phoenix gave us physical, emotional, and spiritual training for India."

Home mission work is excellent training for foreign mission work. The home mission volunteer who develops the essential attitudes of servanthood, openness, and flexibility at home will be better able to exhibit these attitudes on the foreign field.

To be an effective home mission volunteer, you must also understand the difference between doing humanitarian work and ministering. We hear each day of athletes, doctors, members of civic clubs, and concerned neighbors who help victims of poverty or disaster. What sets the home mission volunteer apart from these altruistic individuals?

Foremost, you must realize you are a servant of God. You are not going on a home mission project to rescue someone, to do your civic duty, or to do good deeds. You are going into the situation because the love of Christ compels you to reach out to others. You are going with the intention of laying aside your own rights and allowing God to work through you to touch other lives.

In one church construction project in south Florida, a pastor said, "Volunteers who come to help should come with a servant's heart, expecting nothing in return, and not demanding recognition." This statement may seem harsh to a volunteer who is giving up vacation time and cash to help on a home mission project, but having a servant's heart is essential for effective home mission work.

If you need warm fuzzy feelings and strokes for doing good deeds, avoid home mission projects. Any uplifting emotions should come out of the knowledge that you are doing the will of God, not that you are a hero to the people. Home mission service is a ministry, not a humanitarian work.

Spiritual preparation is as vital to home mission service as to foreign service. In a foreign culture, volunteers quickly realize their own deficiencies and cry out to God for help. In the home culture, however, volunteers tend to keep plowing ahead through difficulties, confident that they can handle the situation.

Macro Journaling

Now is a good time to start your journal. Write down how you came to a decision to volunteer for mission service. In the weeks to come, you may get discouraged about going. Rereading your journal notes will encourage you and help you stay on track.

Even if you hate writing and don't express yourself well, you can preserve a record of your experiences and thoughts with macro journaling.

When you create macros on the computer, you can use a single keystroke to print out several lines of information. In the same way, you can enter phrases in your journal which will trigger a flood of memories when you reread the entries months or even years later.

Use a small spiral notebook (7¾-by-5). Don't worry about proper spelling or sentences. This journal isn't for posterity, but for your personal reference. If you don't know how to start, just make notes on places, weather, people, and events.

For example your journal might read: 1/20—Heard Rod Adams—Talked about Africa—Wish I could go. 1/27—Group from church going to Haiti in June.—Got info on tour—Camping on seacoast—Sounds like my kind of tour. Asked Sam about taking vacation in June. OK with him—Pam doesn't want to go, but wants me to go. 2/10—Did it! Took big jump of faith—Sent in registration yesterday—Got passport photos today—Hate spending money for passport—Am I crazy!? Throwing away my money? Wasting vacation time?

On the field, your entries might read: 6/23 A.M.—Jacmel—church—people crammed in—10 verse songs—people in windows—old man played bass drum. P.M.—Hike in mountains—waterfall, swam in pool, brrrr! 6/24—Woke up to conch shell blowing. Strong smell of charcoal pits burning. Lebien climbed tree, got coconut. Liked coconut water. Scooped coconut meat out with spoon carved from shell—slimy!!—Hungry for pizza—I miss Pam. P.M. Bright sun—no clouds—Hot!—Wedding procession on road. Bride, in white, rode a mule. Everyone dressed up. Men in 3-piece suits. Hot! Children threw poinciana blossoms. Tambourines and flutes. Hot! Sun is searing. P.M. Clear night—rode in back of truck—falling stars—Wish Pam could be with me tonight—Want to come back and bring her.

Five minutes of note taking will produce these little three- or four-word phrases. Years from now, these notes will be like macro keys. Hit one phrase and two pages of memories will print out in your mind. You will increase long-term benefits of your mission tour by observing and recording your observations.

Educate Yourself

Take time to educate yourself about the country and its people. Check out a couple of books from your library or scan old *National Geographic* magazines. Look for adventure stories (fiction and nonfiction) which are set in the country you plan to visit. Buy a travel guide. The more you know about the country and its people, the more you'll enjoy your trip.

CHAPTER 8

Wardrobe

It Does Make a Difference

Whether you are involved in a home or foreign mission project, what you wear does make a difference. In all circumstances, be sure your clothes are modest. Follow the sponsoring organizations' interpretation of modesty. When choosing a wardrobe, keep in mind the climate and altitude. Remember, seasons are reversed in southern hemispheres. At high elevations, nights can be cool even when you are near the equator. Temperatures will drop approximately 3 to 4 degrees for every thousand feet of elevation. Since travel will often take you from one extreme climate to another within hours, layering is the best way to dress. For example, snow flurries pepper the 14,000-foot high plains of La Paz, Bolivia, where the airport is located. However, you may stay in mission accommodations in the lower elevations of La Paz, where palm trees and cacti grow. The amount of clothing you need to take will also depend on available laundry service. Probably the most important item to purchase ahead of time is walking shoes. If the country is underdeveloped, you'll probably feel more comfortable with an enclosed shoe, because of litter and open sewage. Be sure to break in shoes ahead of time. You will need four basic wardrobes. Don't panic! Some sections of the wardrobe only require one set of clothes and they can be used for dual purposes. The basic wardrobes are: international travel, sight-seeing, church, and work.

The way you dress plays an important role in linking cultures. To understand the role of dress, we must understand differences in cultural attitudes toward dress.

In North American culture, our dress makes a statement about our wealth, personality, and stylishness. Dress is a statement of our opinion of ourselves. In many other cultures, the way we dress reflects our view of the people we visit. It is a statement of our opinion of others.

Since clothing is a statement of personal affluence to Americans, many team members have tried to build rapport on the mission field by wearing faded jeans and sneakers to Sunday morning worship. Nationals know that Americans have better clothes and this practice of dressing down sends a negative statement to them. In the past, many team members have even worn their oldest clothes to the mission field, then left them as parting gifts. This practice may have gratified North Americans who were eager to give, and pleased nationals who were eager to receive, but these actions do not build mutual respect which is necessary to bridge cultures.

Here They Come!

Before airport security was tightened in Haiti, my husband and I had our first glimpse of teams from the observation deck. Team members usually stood out in the crowd disembarking from the plane. They approached the terminal with flopping cameras, swiveling heads, and loud conversation. Many of the men wore jeans, work boots, mission logo T-shirts, and caps emblazoned with the names of seed companies. Some girls came in T-shirts, long cotton skirts, and sneakers.

One missionary said, "The problem is that teams think that the country is so poor, that they don't want to come too spiffy. They don't realize that the people here dress in ruffles and frills to go to the airport."

International Travel

Your ministry begins as you enter the country. When you pass through immigration and customs, you are making a statement about your relationship to the country. You will be treated in accordance.

The pleasure-seeking, money-spending tourist who arrives in shorts, gold chains, and flashing diamonds, says to a national, "I'm here on vacation. Make me happy. I'm here to be pleased." The national smiles and takes the tourist's money.

The sloppily dressed team member says, "You are so poor. I feel so sorry for you. I have come to help you poor people." The actions of both the pleasure-seeking tourist and the pitying, mission tourist may help the economy, but neither tourist will forge bonds of respect.

As you enter the country, seek to blend with the residents of the nation. Team members need not come dressed in suits and silk dresses, but they should dress as if they are getting ready to eat at a moderately-priced restaurant.

Avoid anything reflecting the drug scene. Men with earrings, backpacks, extremely long hair, and ragged jeans will get a shakedown even if their T-shirt reads "Jesus is the Rock." Women with stringy hair, unpressed cotton dresses, and ragged-looking sandals are asking for unnecessary searches and questions. Matching T-shirts and hats are acceptable to identify youth groups, but badges are better for adults. T-shirts with suggestive slogans and military fatigues or camouflage suits are always out of place on a mission team.

The more you blend with the international travelers in appearance and conduct, the better impression you will make on immigration and customs officials. Remember, missionaries deal with these officials constantly. Your conduct as a mission team representative can either strengthen or weaken that relationship.

Sight-seeing

While on sight-seeing trips, in resort areas, hotels, and even in missionary housing, almost any type of sensible, modest dress is acceptable. In tourist areas, go ahead and look like a tourist, but always stay within the bounds of what the mission organization considers appropriate.

Work and Contact with the National Church

Appropriate clothing varies according to country and locale within that culture. For the most part, developed nations have a more relaxed dress code than underdeveloped nations; cities are more relaxed than rural areas. The more remote the area, the more removed from western dress code.

In some countries men may wear shorts on the work site. Young men often pull off their shirts when working in the sun, but most missionaries would prefer that they wear a T-shirt. On construction jobs, jeans are usually acceptable for women; in some remote areas, they are not. Shorts are seldom appropriate for women. Women will find a split skirt the most comfortable and acceptable dress in questionable situations. The work project is a great place for adults to wear those matching T-shirts and baseball hats.

During social events with members of the local church, dress casually but not sloppily. As a rule, women should not wear pants to church functions. If in doubt, ask.

After a day of sight-seeing in Guatemala, I returned with a team to the missionary's home. We had just enough time to unload suitcases and head to the church for a farewell evening service and cook out. Since the church was located in Guatemala City, the congregation composed of young families, and the service casual, I assumed that the women on the team could wear pants. I had noted that many of the Guatemalan young women wore pants. To be on the safe side, I checked with the missionary. "No," she answered, "pants will not be appropriate. Please tell the women on the team to wear dresses or skirts. Some young women in the church do wear pants, but this would be offensive to many older members."

Sunday Finery
Always seek the advice of the missionaries you are working with about appropriate dress. In some places dressing up for Sunday services may not be appropriate, while in other places it would be inappropriate not to dress up for Sunday church services.

In many countries, people only have one good outfit, but they wear it when they visit friends and when they attend church. In remote villages, women will walk to church barefoot or wear old shoes, then put on a pair of heels for the church service. Men will wear three-piece suits and ties to thatch-roofed churches in tropical zones.

Again, when dressing up is required, you don't need suits and silk dresses. Men should have dress slacks, shirt, shoes, and tie. If they plan to speak, they should take a sports jacket.

Women should wear dresses, or skirts and blouses, and dress shoes. Dresses or blouses should have at least a cap sleeve. Avoid fabrics which will damage easily, as many pews are made of unfinished wood. Wear dress shoes, but avoid high or narrow heels, because you may have to walk long distances and because rough terrain will ruin those shoes. With the change of a shirt or blouse, the "international travel outfit" can serve as a church outfit. In tropical climates, women seldom wear hose.

Don't Try to Bend the Rules
One team had a few hours to spare before their plane left Miami, so they went to the beach. They raced to board their plane and arrived on the mission field in beach attire. Since it was Christmas season, flights were heavily booked and their luggage didn't arrive. The team was scheduled to leave early the next day on a six-hour trip to the town where they would work. Some team members looked at this as an excuse to bypass the prohibition against working in shorts. In the small town where they were to build a clinic, however, wearing swim trunks to work would

offend the townspeople. That night the missionary dug through "missionary barrels" and through his family's personal belongings to find acceptable clothes for the team members.

Even when mission projects are located on picture postcard, perfect islands, and your travel itinerary promises a chance to snorkel, dive, and sun on powdery beaches, please don't step off the plane in swim trunks.

Dress Code

- Women should dress modestly and avoid provocative, tight, skimpy clothing. Be sure to follow team guidelines.
- Avoid flashy jewelry, even if it's inexpensive.
- Wear clean comfortable clothes, but not fancy clothes. One leader said, "If you can't sit on the floor and get it dirty, leave it at home."
- Avoid expensive name brand clothing, athletic shoes, and purses.
- Don't wear or take anything you can't afford to lose.

Make It Easy on Yourself

If you are purchasing new shirts, skirts, or split skirts, make sure they have pockets. Women who are on work teams will especially need pockets, because purses will be locked in a safe place during work hours.

If you plan to have laundry done, mark your laundry. Jeans, underwear, T-shirts, and socks should be marked. You don't have to put three-inch initials on your clothes as some team members have done. Initials can be placed on the size labels. Socks can be marked by sewing a couple small loops of contrasting thread on the cuff or toe.

Above all, when deciding on your wardrobe, follow the dress code suggested by the host organization.

CHAPTER 9

Packing: Essentials and Nonessentials

What Should I Take?

No one packing list is right for everyone. Packing varies according to type of tour, climate, and individual needs. My husband travels light. Three or four changes of clothes, a toiletry kit, a pair of work shoes, and a Bible completes his packing list. I pack heavier.

Using guidelines supplied by the tour organization, and the suggestions that follow, make a packing list that will meet your needs. The following suggestions include both necessities for travel survival and niceties for travel comfort.

1. Basic wardrobe: Follow mission guidelines.

2. Climate- or work-related clothing: Coats, raincoats, jacket, umbrella, etc. Work teams need gloves.

3. Shoes: Take a comfortable pair to walk and work in, and a pair of dress shoes. Women may also want a pair of sandals or flats.

4. **Hat:** If you're fair-complexioned or bald, take a hat. Hats may be purchased in any country, but you may not go shopping for several days.

5. **Towels:** Unless you have motel or hotel accommodations, take a towel.

6. **Washcloths:** North Americans use washcloths. In other countries, you'll seldom find them in hotels or homes. Always pack a couple of washcloths if you are traveling outside the US.

7. **Basic toiletries and makeup:** Take whatever you use regularly—toothbrush, toothpaste, soap, shampoo, lotions, razor, moisturizer, etc.

8. **Sunscreen and suntan oil:** If you travel to the tropics or a higher altitude, be sure to pack sunscreen. Even tanned Floridians get sunburned at these locations.

9. **Lip balm with sunscreen:** Air travel, as well as exposure to the sun and wind will dry your lips.

10. **Insect repellent:** Repellent will reduce chances of contracting diseases transmitted by insects. Individually packaged wipes with insect repellent are nice. You can tuck them into a pocket or purse.

11. **Bible/Pen/Notebook**

12. **Tissues or handkerchiefs:** Handkerchiefs are better in hot climates. If you use tissues to wipe off sweat, they disintegrate.

13. **Toilet tissue:** If you find toilet tissue in a public rest room, it will probably be poor quality. In many places, you'll be lucky to even find a public rest room.

14. **Talcum powder:** If you do manual work in hot, humid climates, you may have a problem with chafing. In tropical areas you may not wear socks all the time. Sprinkle powder in your shoes to keep feet drier.

15. **Malaria pills** (if needed)

16. **Prescription medicines and over-the-counter remedies:** Be sure to take extra in case return trip is delayed. **Always** keep medications in original containers or pharmaceutical

packets. This will eliminate unnecessary hassles in both the foreign country and the US about possession of drugs or controlled substances.

17. **Antidiarrheals:** No matter how well food and water are monitored, you may still get diarrhea. Some people are more sensitive to water changes than others. This does not mean that you have gotten contaminated water, or food, but rather you have picked up a bacteria which is foreign to your body. Foreign travelers have the same problem when they travel in North America. Another cause of diarrhea is eating too much fresh fruit. Teams coming from cold climates in the winter time often overindulge in fresh tropical fruits. If you have a sensitive system, take an antidiarrheal along, or ask your doctor for a prescription of some other strong, fast-acting medicine.

18. **Laxative:** Travel and a change in schedule may create the opposite problem for some team members. If constipation is a common problem for you, toss in a packet of laxative gum or some bran tablets.

19. **Small closeable plastic bags:** Take three or four bags for wet washcloths, garbage, leaky bottles, etc.

20. **Plastic grocery bags:** Take three or four to pack dirty clothes and shoes on return trip.

21. **Flashlight:** A small one is fine. Be sure batteries are fresh.

22. **Watch:** Everyone needs a timepiece. If you do not have a watch, get a two-dollar, stick-up clock and carry it in a pocket.

23. **Swimsuit/beach towel:** This will depend on tour agenda and mission policy. Skimpy swimsuits are never acceptable for either men or women.

24. **Travel alarm** (battery operated)

25. **Adhesive bandages, antiseptic, and antibacterial ointment:** In the tropics, wounds get infected easily.

26. **Camera/film:** Take three or four more rolls of film than you expect to use. Put in a fresh light meter battery. If possible take zoom and wide-angle lenses. If you take a video recorder, be sure to take extra power packs and an AC adapter. (Some

countries in Asia and Africa forbid the use of video cameras. Ask before taking one.)

27. **Wet wipes:** Great for washing hands before eating. Sanitary washrooms are hard to find. Individually wrapped wipes are easier to carry. Members of work teams will find washcloth-size baby wipes handy for quick cleanups. Using these will help cut down on the spread of disease.

Don't Expect to Shop

The best packing rule to remember is, *Don't plan to go shopping— even if your mission trip is in the US.* Take what you need. If you have your own transportation and have free time to wander around a mall, that's fine; but don't make shopping for toiletries and snacks a part of your tour agenda.

If you have your own recreational vehicle and travel often, you'll be fairly well prepared for your trip. If, however, you seldom travel or plan to stay in dormitory-type facilities, glance through the Packing Checklist at the end of chapter 10 for packing suggestions.

The Next Time I'll Take . . .

The following aren't necessities, but you may wish you had included them.

Handheld tape recorder/empty tapes: Music lovers will enjoy taping the sounds of homemade instruments, new rhythms, and familiar songs done in a different language. Some recordings could be used as background for your mission presentation when you return home.

Calculator: Slip a credit-card-size calculator into your wallet. It will make figuring currency exchange easier.

Electrical adapter: If electrical current is different, you may need an adapter to run electric razors and hair dryers, and to recharge power packs for video recorders.

Altimeter: This is definitely a nonessential, but fun item. If you're traveling in the Andes or some other major mountain chain, you may enjoy taking a small, handheld altimeter. Even in the lower ranges of Central America, we found team members had a lot of fun calling out the altitude as we ascended and descended through clouds.

Phrase book or electronic translator: A phrase book is adequate, but if you enjoy spending money on electronic gadgets you'll enjoy a translator. Translators come in two basic types: dictionaries and phrase books. If you have some knowledge of the language's structure, you can use the dictionary. If you have little or no foreign language skills, you'll be better off with a phrase translator.

Married Couples

If accommodations are in a hotel or motel, and you have a private bath, pack as you would for any other vacation trip. If accommodations are in a home or church, or in dorm-type facilities, you may sleep in all-men or all-women rooms. You may also share a bathroom with several team members. If you do not have a private bath, pack separate suitcases. Be sure each person has a complete set of basic toiletries. This will eliminate shouting through a closed door trying to get a spouse's attention, and waiting until everyone in the room is either decent or out of view so that the shampoo can be handed out to you.

Cut Out the Suffering

When my husband packs, he packs only necessities. I prepare for every emergency I can anticipate. I have "learned to suffer," but I don't suffer unnecessarily.

If you don't "suffer well," you may want to include some of the following items.

1. Copy of a favorite devotional. Team members usually have daily devotions together. If you aren't used to public speaking, photocopy a one-page favorite devotional you can read.
2. Addresses. If you plan to send postcards, don't take an address book. Put the addresses you need on a file card.
3. Earplugs. Don't laugh. Someone gave me a set of soft foam earplugs to wear while flying on a DC-3. I didn't wear them on the plane, but when the disco in the hotel in which we stayed started blasting music at 1:00 A.M., I used the earplugs. I think

I was the only team member who slept well during that tour. If you're a light sleeper, and have accommodations in a city, a set of soft foam earplugs (don't get hard swimming plugs) will eliminate a lot of 2:00 to 5:00 A.M. suffering.

4. A daily tote. Whenever you go out for the day, you'll want to keep several items with you such as ID, money, sunscreen, camera, snacks, wet wipes, etc. Your camera bag or carry-on will probably work. If the carry-on is too big, or camera bag too

---

Communal Bathrooms

If you share a bathroom, or if accommodations are in a dorm or camping setting, take modest sleepwear and a tote bag (plastic bag is fine) to carry your towel, toiletries, and change of clothes to the bathroom. Also take flip-flops, because shower areas are often muddy and mildewed.

Contact Lens Wearers

Take liquid tears, a contact case, and a pair of glasses. On long flights, take out your contact lenses. In the zero humidity of aircraft cabins, soft contact lenses (especially the disposable ones) will dry out, and may even adhere to the cornea.

On the ground, you will often travel in open-window vehicles or in the back of trucks. Liquid tears will usually alleviate any discomfort from wind and dust, but take a pair of glasses just in case you get into a high-dust situation. In some countries, during dry season, the dust is plowed from the road like snow. Under such conditions, riding in the back of a pickup truck while wearing contacts would be impossible.

Protective Packing

Use zipper-storage bags or sealed plastic containers for suntan oil, lotions, perfumes, aftershaves, and cremes in jars. If you use softside luggage, be sure that any breakable, hard plastic items such as blow-dryers or bottles are protected from crushing.

small, take a small duffel-type nylon bag that packs flat and doesn't take up room in your suitcase. For security reasons, be sure that the duffel will zip shut.

5. If you have problems with blood sugar or must have meals at set times, take along packs of granola bars, peanut butter and crackers, or cheese and crackers. Always have some in your daily tote. Travel delays are common. Since most travel must be done in daytime hours due to road hazards, long trips are made with few stops.

6. If you are accustomed to eating snacks, take some. Don't expect to buy snacks after you arrive. When taking snacks, take cans rather than bags of chips, and seal chocolate in tight containers. (Coated chocolate such as M&M candies travel better.) If you plan to stay in a missionary home, take candy for the missionary family. Missionaries who haven't seen a Snickers candy bar for two years have trouble coping with empty Snickers wrappers in the waste can.

7. If you have recurring problems with sinuses, allergies, asthma, hemorrhoids, headaches, or blisters on the mouth, take along any over-the-counter remedies or prescriptions that you commonly use. Heavy air pollution in cities and pollen and dust in the country may produce allergies and sinus problems. Extreme sun, wind, and cold may trigger headaches and blisters.

8. Motion sickness: Unless you're sailing on high seas or riding a bus through the Andes, or you have an unusually sensitive stomach, you won't need motion sickness medicine. If you do take motion sickness medicine, use a nondrowsy type. If you sleep during travel time, you'll miss an important part of your tour.

Am I Taking Too Much?

The best known packing rule is "pack what you think you'll need and leave half behind." Some people will go on mission tours without any of the extras and have a great trip. I know that I probably pack too much, but I have more peace of mind if I include the extras. As you decide what to take, remember flying and change of climate often trigger physical discomforts. Your body will adjust in a couple days, but if you haven't traveled much, or you "don't suffer well," a little advance preparation will make those first few days easier.

In an emergency almost any of the extra preparation items can be purchased in any country of the world—if you know where to find them and if you have the time to go get them. Remember, however, drugstores aren't always around the corner. Even travel to a developed country does not ensure easy access to shopping. Furthermore, unscheduled stops for film, hats, aspirin, and snacks limit the efficiency of a team. If every member on the team requests one stop, that may add up to 20 unnecessary breaks in the schedule. Take whatever you anticipate as reasonable needs.

With the exception of snacks, all the extras will require minimal space in your suitcase. All the extra prescriptions and over-the-counter remedies that you will need will probably fit into a sandwich bag.

You may never use some of the extras, but you'll relax more knowing you are prepared. You'll also become a favorite with those on the tour who aren't so well prepared.

Women Only

Simplify your beauty routine. A simple hairstyle that doesn't require a blow-dryer or curling iron is best. Be able to shower, do hair, and apply makeup in a half-hour. Look good, but not great. You will probably be sharing bathroom facilities, and the schedule will be crowded. A day or two may be set aside for sight-seeing, but side trips are often crammed in between other activities. Fifteen team members do not want to lose an hour's sight-seeing because three members take too long dressing.

Take along an adequate supply of feminine products. Stress and excitement can change body rhythms. If you cross a time zone, don't change the timing of birth control pills. Keep on your old schedule. If you commonly have yeast infections or cystitis, take along medication. (Some medicines for malaria may encourage yeast infections or decrease effectiveness of birth control pills. If in doubt, check with your doctor.) Panty liners and personal cleansing towels can help you feel fresh on long travel days.

Be prepared for different toilet facilities and little privacy. Avoid jumpsuits and bodysuits. Skirts are the most modest when there are no bathroom facilities. In hot climates wear cotton underwear. Washcloth-size baby wipes are great for quick cleanups when there is no water.

If you do manual labor, be sure to take gloves. Take cotton bandannas for wiping sweat. Also take a small nail brush and basic manicure set. If you must take nail polish, never take bottles or jars of nail polish remover. They almost always leak. Take polish remover wipes. If you must have a curling iron but electricity will not be available, get a butane iron. You'll find those in camping supplies.

Take a simple scarf. In some cultures, women are expected to cover their heads in church.

Airline Travel

If traveling by commercial airline, you will usually have more luggage allowance than you need. Do, however, try to limit personal belongings to one carry-on and one checked bag. For a ten-day trip, all necessary and extra preparedness items should fit into one large suitcase (70 pounds, 62 inches) and a carry-on.

Don't take a bag so large that you can't handle it easily. Limiting your baggage to a carry-on and one large checked piece serves two purposes.

1. Less luggage will be easier for you to manage in crowded vehicles and crowded sleeping rooms.
2. Your extra baggage allowance will permit the mission agency to send in requested items and project-related materials without paying excess baggage charges.

Missionary Flights

All or a portion of your transportation may be in a small mission plane. On a small plane be sure to adhere strictly to weight limitations. If you exceed your limit on a commercial airline, you might have to pay excess baggage fees. If you exceed your allowance on a small plane, part of your belongings **will be left behind.**

If flying by small plane, reduce weight by using nylon or canvas duffel bags, backpacks, or sports bags. To further cut weight, pack travel-size toiletries and double up with others on items you can share (blow-dryers, first-aid items, etc.).

CHAPTER 10

Special Preparations and Packing Instructions

Do It Now

Make a checklist of all the items needed for your particular ministry or work project. If you plan to borrow tools, musical instruments, or any other equipment, make sure those arrangements are confirmed well in advance of departure. Musical instruments or delicate medical equipment which will not fit into overhead luggage compartments on plane should be packed in shockproof cases or packages. Either locate a case or construct one well ahead of time.

If you plan a craft activity for children, make sure that you have **every** item needed. Don't expect to buy anything on the mission field. Almost any item can be obtained in any country of the world; however, finding the item will waste time and cost more money. One team had every item for craft projects, except sponges. "I didn't have time to buy sponges," the craft coordinator said. "We'll just pick some up in Guatemala City." What would have been a simple purchase in the States ended up being a half-day, fruitless search for the Guatemalan architect who had to leave the construction project to search for sponges. Shopping in many countries is like shopping in scattered flea markets. Unless you know which flea market and exactly which vendor sells a particular item, you must search through endless alleys and stalls before finding the item.

It's also better to cut out crafts ahead of time. Teams that stay up until 1:00 A.M. cutting out crafts and then roll out of bed at 6:00 A.M., get grumpy. Some team members love keeping late hours but those who are forced—as part of a team—to stay up and help resent the lack of preparation by craft coordinators. If you are responsible for assembling materials for crafts, complete the work before departure. Ask family, friends, and church members to help. It's an early way to link the home church to the mission field.

Children's activities are conducted on the mission field in either controlled or uncontrolled settings. Controlled groups are in schools, orphanages, and day-care facilities. Teachers who know the children and deal daily with them will assist you. Uncontrolled settings are open to the public. They include church Vacation Bible Schools or open-air Bible clubs. If you plan a craft for an uncontrolled situation, place the parts for individual crafts in sandwich bags. You can then easily distribute a packet to each child rather than trying to figure out if each child has all the needed parts.

Members of medical teams should check about the necessity of sending professional documents in advance. In some countries, documents must be sent several months ahead of time in order to get government clearance. Always take a copy of credentials with you.

Even though slightly outdated medicine may seem to be better than no medicine, customs officials will often dump it. Don't try to take it in unless you know for sure that it will be accepted.

Requested Items

If you are traveling on commercial airlines, you probably won't need all your luggage allowance. Usually, team members limit their belongings to one checked bag and a carry-on. You can use the extra luggage allowance for items that the missionaries have requested or suggested. On the return trip, use the extra baggage allowance for souvenirs.

Food Pantry Items

Mixes (cakes, cookies, brownies, cheesecakes, etc.)
Frostings for mixes
Seasoning mixes (taco, sloppy joes, sour cream, dips)
Salad dressing packets (include some low calorie)
Powdered drink mixes
Gelatins, puddings (basic flavors)
Tea bags (regular, decaffeinated, and specialty flavors)
Instant coffee (regular and decaffeinated)
Hot chocolate mix
Nuts
Popcorn
Whipped topping mix
Chocolate candy (pack unsealed candy in plastic bags)

Among the packing suggestions from the mission organization, you may find a list of food pantry items. These items are either hard to find in the country or very expensive. If such a list is not included, you might consider taking some food pantry items anyway.

If the mission organization asks you to take in specific items, such as auto parts, or if missionaries request special items, they should reimburse you. Be sure to keep all receipts. You may also need them in customs.

Getting Personal

You may choose to help missionaries on the field in a personal way. Music tapes, CDs, videos, books, magazines, 35mm film (good grade—bargain film fades), cosmetics, or hobby-related items are appreciated. If you duplicate a book or tape which they already have, they will pass it on to another missionary family. One team member brought us a recipe for a special dessert and the ingredients to make it three times. Don't forget MKs. Missionaries' kids love trendy items—hats, T-shirts, posters, CDs, video games, etc. Again, involve others in your church in preparation. Ask if anyone wants to contribute to a surprise package for the missionary family.

No! Not the Kitchen Sink!

Don't clean out your cabinets. One couple literally took the kitchen sink. They cleaned cabinets and took everything from individual packets of ketchup to outdated clothing—and, they took a chipped sink that they had removed from their home during remodeling. No matter how impoverished a nation is, it is not a dumping station. **Do not** gather up the items you couldn't sell in your garage sale and take to the mission field. As a rule, if you wouldn't use it yourself, don't take it.

Don't think cheap. Think usefulness and quality. Ask missionaries and mission organizations what they need. **Meet needs.**

Do not purchase gifts and candy to pass out to children or people with whom you will work. Most missions have strict policies about handouts. Do not buy school supplies unless you know what is specifically needed. School paper is ruled differently in other countries.

Roll Those Cameras Now

Additional preparation includes testing new or borrowed equipment. If you borrow cameras or video recorders, get them in advance and experiment. Team members often finish the first roll of film and can't remember how to reload the camera.

Take a few photos of yourself and your family in scenic settings near your home. These will be good to show friends you meet on the field. It will give them an idea of where and how you live. Avoid photos that display your personal material possessions: house, car, boat. Take photos which show universal possessions: family, hometown, church, natural surroundings.

If you will be staying in a private home, you may want to take a small gift. It isn't necessary to take a gift to missionaries, but they do appreciate books, tapes, or practical items. If staying in a national's home, take time to choose an attractive, American item that can be displayed. Look at craft shows for an item which clearly speaks of your own culture. If possible find something that has your hometown or home state tastefully inscribed on the front or back. When presenting it, explain the piece of America that the item represents.

Duty-free Packing

It would be easier to pack your personal items in one suitcase and requested items in a second. If you take in gifts or requested items however, you will need to follow specific guidelines to eliminate unnecessary customs fees.

Some volunteers fear they are being deceptive and dishonest by following these prescribed guidelines. On the contrary, these packing guidelines keep the volunteer from giving a false impression and being mistaken for a merchandiser.

Merchandisers travel to North America, buy thousands of dollars worth of new merchandise, fly back to their own country, and turn the merchandise over to a merchant for resale. Merchandise which is purchased abroad for resale is subject to customs taxes.

Mission teams do not carry in merchandise that will be resold. A single suitcase packed with food and new items, however, might appear to be that of a merchandiser, and might subject you to unnecessary hassles in customs. If items are distributed among your own things, they will appear as reasonable purchases for your personal use and for friends you may visit in the country.

To eliminate unnecessary customs questions and unnecessary duty, follow these guidelines:

1. Take items out of plastic wrappers and remove extra packaging. This doesn't mean that you take pudding out of its box, but you would take a tube of toothpaste out of a box. You would remove the plastic wrapper from a tape or CD, but not remove the CD from the case. You would take a small appliance out of the box. If the box has essential information printed on it, fold it flat and place it between towels or clothing.
2. Remove all price tags, especially from tools, toys, entertainment items, small appliances, and clothes. Put the price tickets with the receipts in an envelope and place in your carry-on. If duty is levied, you'll need to show the price tags in customs; you'll also need these for reimbursement from the missionary.
3. Distribute special purchases among your personal items.
4. Do not gift wrap any item. If you plan to gift wrap, take paper and tape and do it after you arrive.

Packing in this manner is not a type of deception or an attempt to bypass a custom's law. It simply eliminates unnecessary explanations and possible seizure. For you, unpacking will be a mess. You'll find extras in your personal belongings for days after you arrive, but it's the best way to avoid paying unnecessary duty.

First-Aid Kit

A well-organized tour will provide a first-aid kit for a team. Many tours, however, do not. If you have medical training, put together a small first-aid kit. If you are traveling into a remote area where there is no local clinic, include stethoscope, blood pressure cuff, needles, syringes, sutures, splints, and several pairs of latex gloves. You may not use all of the items in the packet, but the team members will feel more comfortable knowing that first-aid items are available. Leave any unused items with a missionary or national health worker.

Art Lovers, Prepare to Bring Home a Find

If you enjoy picking up unusual souvenirs that may not fit in your luggage, use nesting luggage, and take a roll of strapping tape. On the return trip, eliminate one piece of luggage by cramming personal belongings inside a smaller suitcase and placing it inside a larger one. Use the extra luggage allowance for a painting, wood carving, etc. You can fashion a carrying case for your souvenir with cardboard from boxes and strapping tape.

Group Travel

Cut packing by doubling up with other team members on items such as: first-aid kit, electrical adapter, canister of wet wipes, toilet tissue, strapping tape, blow-dryer, curling iron.

Leave It at Home

1. **Jewelry:** Unless you plan dinner with the prime minister or other dignitaries, keep jewelry simple. Don't take anything that you can't wear all the time; or if you leave it off, that you can't afford to lose. Don't rely on hotel safes to keep your valuables protected.
2. **Leather jackets:** When Jim boarded the first leg of his flight to

Jamaica, in Pittsburgh, he wore a leather jacket. In Jamaica, he folded the jacket and placed it on the floor beside his suitcase. In the night, a rat chewed holes in the jacket. When traveling from a cold climate to a low altitude tropical climate, give your coats—especially leather ones—to friends at the airport.

3. **Radios:** Leave boom boxes and tapes at home unless you use them in ministry. Focus on the sounds of the country you're visiting rather than on the sounds of your own culture.

4. **Charge cards:** As a rule, leave all but a major charge card, an ATM card, and a phone card at home. You won't have any use for your Home Depot or J. C. Penney card, so don't run the risk of losing them.

Insurance

Take your insurance identification card and a claim form. In case of a claim, you'll want to have information filled out and signed by the physician immediately, rather than trying to do it by correspondence later.

Why Not Help the Needy Here?

When friends and relatives realize that you are going to go through with this insane urge to visit the mission field, they may decide it is their duty to bring you to your senses. It happens to everyone who goes to the mission field, even to veteran missionaries. Surprisingly, many negative comments will come from church members.

Among the comments and questions you will hear are: Why go there? There are plenty of needs right here at home. Wouldn't it be better to send the money to the mission field than waste it on a trip? Aren't you afraid?

Everyone will suddenly start giving you news clippings of every disease, murder, and weather change in that country. Someone will have a neighbor of a friend of an uncle's wife who almost, nearly, just about had an accident in that country.

You may encounter genuine personal hindrances relating to your work and family. Don't get discouraged or give up on the trip. You made a prayerful and rational decision believing this was a good time to visit the mission field. Concentrate on dealing with any real problems and ignore the *what if's* that arise. Some people back out at the last moment because of vague fears. Pinpoint your fears. Are they based on reality or are they natural apprehensions which accompany any stretching experience? Our greatest fear is that we will meet something unexpected that is too big for us to handle. Don't forget, you are going to do a spiritual work, and God is bigger than any situation you will encounter.

Eliminate as many worries as possible in your personal life by preparing ahead of time for the care of your family, business, house, pets, plants, and whatever else may need perpetual care in your life.

If a last minute barrier crashes across your path, present your need to God in prayer, as well as to friends or the church body. Others may be able to help you. If the way still seems closed to you, accept it and plan to go another time. We don't always understand closed doors, but at times we need to accept them.

An Indiana couple usually spent two weeks each winter working on mission construction projects. One year, they made plans as usual, but a series of problems kept them from going. They tried to work around the problems but finally canceled their reservation. During the time that they were scheduled to travel with the team, the man suffered a bowel blockage. Fast action by surgeons saved his life. Immediate medical care would not have been available on the scheduled mission tour.

Your trip can be canceled due to political upheaval, natural disaster, or illness of team leaders or missionaries. Cancellation can occur at any time—even after you have arrived at the airport. Although you may be disappointed, accept the change of plans as coming through the hands of a gracious God. Consider a cancellation a delay, not an end of your plans to visit the mission field.

Session Two
Individual or Group Assignments

Discovery Questions and Activities

1. Take time to get better acquainted with teammates. Choose someone who you do not know well and find out what they do for recreation or relaxation. Ask about what they would like to do, if they had money and courage to do it (skydiving, auto racing, acting, etc.). Discuss what you discovered about each other. Were you surprised by your findings? How did your findings compare with your initial impression of the person?

2. Decide if you'll be helping the missionary in a personal way. If you don't know the missionary, write asking about ages of children, hobbies, and tastes in books and music. If you offer to make purchases for the missionary, make it clear whether you will be paying for the items or you will expect to be reimbursed. If you have limited funds, you might write, "I will have some extra luggage allowance. If you would like me to make any purchases for you, I would be glad to do so. Don't worry about sending money now. You can pay me when I see you." Allow two months for correspondence to be answered.

3. Start linking your home church to the field by:
   - Getting classes or small groups involved in helping prepare crafts
   - Collecting food pantry items
   - Preparing a missionary care package
   - Asking a nonteam member to be a prayer partner. Pray together at least once a week about the mission tour.

4. Develop a personal foreign language phrase book. Use a 3-by-5 spiral note pad which you can carry in a pocket. Include phrases and words relating to the mission project and to church services. See Common Phrases.

5. Photocopy the checklists at the end of this chapter. Check each item as you complete it. The more items you check off in advance, the more relaxed you'll be the week before departure.

Assignment

Check on your health insurance. Does your health insurance cover you outside of the US? Will it cover emergency medical evacuation? If not, will the mission organization's insurance cover evacuation? Write out your testimony.

Advance Preparation Checklist

Use the following packing checklist to develop your personal checklist.

❑ Registration
❑ Passport
❑ Visas
❑ Immunizations
❑ Basic wardrobe (include comfortable shoes)
❑ Collect special tools or equipment. Provide sturdy carrying cases.

❑ Write out testimony or message.
❑ Complete project preparations which can be done in advance (cut crafts, practice music, etc.).
❑ Purchase items requested by missionary or host organization.
❑ Put together a care package for missionary.
❑ Test new equipment.

Packing Checklist

❑ Toiletries/makeup
❑ Sunscreen
❑ Insect repellent
❑ Lip balm
❑ Toilet tissue
❑ Facial tissue/handkerchiefs
❑ Watch
❑ Sleeping attire/robe
❑ Flip-flops
❑ Towel/washcloths
❑ Jacket/sweater
❑ Snack food
❑ Flashlight
❑ Hat
❑ Work gloves
❑ Camera/film
❑ Video recorder/battery pack
❑ A/C adapter
❑ Tape recorder/tapes
❑ Batteries
❑ Swimsuit/beach towel
❑ Bible/pen/notebook
❑ Basic wardrobe

❑ Sunglasses
❑ Plastic bags (for wet items and dirty laundry)
❑ Mirror
❑ Travel-size phrase book or translator
❑ Phone numbers of home and mission field contacts
❑ Addresses for postcards
❑ Passport/visa
❑ Credentials (medical personnel)
❑ Photos of you and your family
❑ Wet wipes
❑ Travel alarm
❑ Devotional guide
❑ First-aid items—bandages, alcohol swabs, antibacterial ointment, pain killer, diarrhea medicine, laxative, eye drops, cough syrup
❑ Over-the-counter medicines for any recurring illnesses or allergies
❑ Items related to project
❑ Outline of testimony

Common Phrases

Hello _____

Good morning _____

Good evening _____

How are you? _____

How is your family? _____

man _____

woman _____

girl _____

boy _____

thank you _____

excuse me _____

How much is this? _____

How old is he/she? _____

Where do you live? _____

yes _____

no _____

stop _____

go _____

give _____

good-bye _____

please _____

My name is _____

What is your name? _____

today _____

tomorrow _____

yesterday _____

How many children do you have? _____

How much is this? _____

Where is the lavatory (toilet)? _____

I do not understand. _____

I am very happy to meet you. _____

I am very happy to be here. _____

It's beautiful. _____

Please, give me _____

No, thank you. I don't need it now. _____

Praise (glory) be to God. _____

I don't speak _____

Food terms (milk, water, bread, etc.) _____

VBS terms (scissors, pencil, crayon) _____

Tools (hammer, screwdriver, nails) _____

Numbers (1-100) _____

_____

_____

_____

_____

_____

_____

_____

_____

_____

_____

Colors _____

_____

_____

_____

_____

_____

Days of the week _____

_____

_____

_____

PART THREE

Travel and Survival

CHAPTER 11

Last-Minute Details

Emergency Information

Although you've already completed most of your preparations, some details must be left until the last few days.

If you have received a new passport, be sure to sign the inside. Fill the information page out in *pencil*. Include your blood type. If you have had your passport for a while, update emergency contact data. Filling in the foreign address is optional. Make three or four copies of the photo identification page for:

- home—leave one copy with a family member or friend;
- yourself—put a copy in your wallet;
- luggage—put a couple of copies in your luggage or somewhere separate from your passport or billfold.

If you are involved in a home mission project, carry the same type of information in your wallet: your blood type, the address and phone number of a contact at home, and other useful emergency information.

Leave Emergency Information with Your Family or a Friend

- Copy of passport identification page, or the emergency information that you are carrying.
- Itinerary: List airline, flight number, or other transportation information, and key destinations
  For example:
  - Fly to Amsterdam 4/14 Airline/flight number
  - Depart for Nairobi 4/15
  - Nairobi 4/15 to 4/21
  - Depart for Johannesburg 4/22
  - Johannesburg 4/22 to 4/24
  - Fly to Amsterdam 4/25 Airline/flight number
  - Fly to New York 4/26 Airline/flight number
- Phone numbers: Give the phone number and names of principal contacts in the stateside mission organization. If you have a number of the missionary contact in the foreign country, or the number of the place in which you'll be staying, include those numbers, also.

Doing Favors for Friends

A friend or a neighbor may ask you to take a gift for an acquaintance. First, make sure the item is unwrapped and clearly identifiable. Never carry in a wrapped package. You are the one who will be blamed if it contains contraband. Next, **do not** agree to deliver a package. Explain to your friend that you are with a tour group and do not have private transportation. Agree to take the package only to the place where you will be staying. The intended recipient will have to pick it up at that location. Missionaries do not have time to track down strangers or take team members on private excursions to deliver packages.

Unless you have a specific phone number, do not promise to contact the recipient. Making contact without a phone number is nearly impossible; phones are often listed in the names of landlords, not the tenants. Insist that the giver contact the recipient. I made the mistake of offering to take a package to someone in Caracas. It took several weeks and several attempts to deliver the package.

Money

Everyone wants to know how much money and what kind of money to take. It depends on the type of tour. If you have an all-inclusive tour package, you'll only need money for souvenirs and incidental expenses. Half in cash and half in travelers checks should be fine. Get travelers checks in $20 denominations.

If you plan to purchase expensive items such as jewelry, leather goods, electronics, or cameras, take a credit card or travelers checks. Some people adamantly oppose the use of credit cards, but sensible use of a credit card is better than carrying large amounts of cash. People who peel off hundred-dollar bills to settle hotel accounts and to make major purchases are handing out invitations to be robbed.

If you pay all expenses out-of-pocket: hotel, food, travel, etc., take a major credit card, travelers checks, and enough cash for the first two days. Charge hotel and car rental in order to keep from carrying so much money. Use travelers checks to pay for meals in larger restaurants, but have cash for meals in smaller establishments and for inexpensive souvenir purchases.

Team members often wish they had brought more money in order to help the local church. In Guatemala one construction team quickly used all the building materials on hand. One woman used her extra spending money to purchase a load of concrete blocks.

Travelers Checks

Some banks issue two-party travelers checks. These are convenient for couples to use, since either person may sign them. Travelers in some countries, however, have found that cashiers who are unfamiliar with the checks require both people to sign the checks in person. Until the two-party checks are more common worldwide, stick with the standard one-party checks.

You may want to take along extra travelers checks in case you see a need that you can meet.

Individual needs and tastes will further determine how much money you take. You should have adequate information ahead of time to know cost of hotel and ground transportation. If you don't know about food, plan as you would for a North American vacation. If you can afford it, take a few more travelers checks than you plan to spend. It's easier to cash in unused travelers checks than to write a personal check in a foreign country.

Your Most Important Piece of Luggage

Your most important piece of luggage is your carry-on bag. Baggage is often delayed, and sometimes never catches up with you until you get back home. If you pack your carry-on properly, and none of the rest of your luggage ever shows up, you can still have a good trip.

Your carry-on bag should include:
• Change of clothes—appropriate to the type of tour;
• Comfortable shoes;
• Two changes of undergarments and socks;
• Basic toiletries/makeup;
• All prescriptions/medicines;
• Document pouch (see sidebar);
• Any item of sentimental or monetary value that you can't afford to lose: charge cards, camera, tape recorder, Bible, jewelry, etc;
• Emergency rations—three or four granola bars or packages of crackers.

Carrying "emergency rations" is especially important on flight day. Departure in the US may be delayed. The plane may be rerouted because of bad weather. When you arrive, the missionary may need to hastily pack the team into a van and rush to get through checkpoints or ford rivers before dark. In many underdeveloped countries, road hazards make traveling at night dangerous. In situations like this, there will be no stops for food. Getting to a destination safely will overrule murmurs of hunger and thirst. Be prepared with emergency rations.

Avoid Ticket Counter Fumbles

If you don't have a special holder for tickets and documents, you might want to use a bank deposit-type pouch or a 5-by-7 manila envelope. During international travel time, it is important to have tickets, passport, documents, a pen, and a small amount of cash in an easy-to-reach place at all times. Nothing is more frustrating than trying to find a paper while officials are waiting, people in line behind you are pushing, and you are concerned about keeping your luggage safe.

On the outside of the document envelope, or on a file card which is kept in the pouch, make a list of the document pouch items (see sidebar). These items should be in the pouch at all times. Always keep the document pouch in an easy-to-reach place that is secure.

Document Pouch

- Tickets
- Passport/visas
- Phone numbers—home, US mission contact, foreign contact
- Address of place in which you'll stay in foreign country
- $20 in single bills for tips
- Keys to luggage (Put keys in a change envelope to keep them from being pulled out accidentally.)
- Pen

Carry-on Bag Restrictions

Carry-on bag restrictions vary. Sometimes you can board with a carry-on bag, *and* an additional carry-on such as a musical instrument, hanging bag, or briefcase. On some flights, agents may strictly enforce the one-piece limit. Regulations vary with carrier; enforcement depends on flight load on the day you travel and mood of airline agents.

Jeff arrived at the boarding gate just in time to make his flight. Traveling light, he had everything in a backpack which he carried. The steward at the plane door said that the bag would not fit in the overhead compartment, and he would check it for Jeff. Jeff never saw the backpack again.

On a weekend trip, my husband, Dave, packed everything, including a hammer, in a carry-on bag. Security took the hammer and checked it. Dave never saw the hammer again. Although he immediately filed a claim, and made two trips to the Miami airport, his hammer was never recovered.

Dental Work

Avoid dental work 24 hours before a flight. An air bubble trapped in an opened tooth may expand during flight, causing excruciating pain.

Customs Registry

If you are traveling to a country noted for manufacturing or selling cameras, electronic equipment, and watches, you might want to register your own equipment with customs in order to avoid being taxed when you bring it back through customs. To avoid tax, either register items at the customs office in an international airport or have sales receipts for proof of purchase in the US or Canada.

If you're with a group, traveling light, and don't plan to check a bag, put your tools in someone's checked baggage. Also, put pocketknives in checked luggage. Sometimes you can carry them through in your pocket or in a carry-on, but if a knife is taken at a security check, you'll be lucky to see it again. When packing a carry-on make sure that:

- it will fit under the airline seat or in the overhead compartment;
- all items will clear security;
- all carry-ons have identification tags on both the outside and inside, in case they are checked at the gate.

If you anticipate a flight with extremely strict regulations about carry-on bags and you have delicate musical, electronic, or medical instruments, try to get preflight approval to carry them. As last resort, team members may make room for an instrument by squeezing their carry-on items into one bag.

If I Can Call

If you plan to call home, make it clear to your family that you may not be able to reach them. This way, they will not panic if they don't hear from you. If you plan to call, give a general time, "evening or Sunday afternoon," but preface your promise with "if I can call."

Some team members have been upset when they could not call home to reassure families of their safe arrival or to check on their businesses. When taking a mission trip, plan on leaving your personal world behind for the duration of the trip. In an emergency, mission officials will reach either you or your family with important information.

CHAPTER 12

Security Measures

You Are Your Best Security Guard

If you have traveled much or have lived in a major city, the following safety guidelines are second nature to you. I've grown so used to protecting my purse that when I walk into my small-town, home church, I often find my purse tucked under my arm like a football.

The following information will show you how best to protect your money, luggage, and yourself. These guidelines aren't given to frighten you, but rather to help you travel more safely in both North America and other parts of the world.

Security of Money

Tips on keeping your money safe remind me of my mother's advice during a thunderstorm. Wherever I stood in a room, lightning was sure to zap me. Near the door, lightning followed a draft of air; in the center of the room, it would jump from the light fixture; near the wall, it would follow the wall. In her estimation no place was safe from lightning. Still, I had to be somewhere.

In the same way, no matter where or how you decide to carry your money, you run some risk of losing it. Still, you have to carry it somewhere.

Some ways of carrying money are definitely risky. High risk ways of carrying money include:

- Waist bags. In crowds, the belt can easily be snipped. Use these bags for one-day excursions where you don't carry your passport or much money.
- Billfolds in a hip pocket.
- Handle satchel purses. They're hard to hold on to if a purse snatcher grabs them.
- Shoulder bags that hang loosely on the hip. They can easily be pilfered, or the bottom slit and contents removed.

Safer ways to carry money include:

- **Money belts or money pouches.** This is one of the safest ways to carry money. Some are built into men's dress belts, others are worn around the neck or waist, under clothing.
- **Purses.** Some travel magazines advise women never to carry a purse. I find that hard to do. I usually carry a shoulder-strap purse, with the strap over my head and across my body. Depending on the surroundings, I either tuck the purse up under my arm like a football, or I rest my arm on the purse and keep a grip on it. Always make sure compartments are closed. Some women carry a purse around their neck and hanging in front. I find that uncomfortable. It can also be dangerous if a criminal is determined to rob you.
- **Money clips.** Some use money clips and keep their cash in a front pants pocket.
- **Wallet in front pants pocket.** Some place rubber bands around a billfold so that it's harder to slip out of a pocket.
- **Euro man's bag.** Another popular option for carrying money, especially among men, is the Euro bag or man's bag. This is a small leather clutch bag (6 inches-by-10 inches) with a strap

which slips around the wrist. The clutch has space for tickets, passport, travel documents, maps, credit cards, and cash. It is easy to protect and keeps all travel items easily accessible. You'll see many men from other nations carrying these clutches. Before making a remark about men carrying purses, keep in mind that many of these "purses" contain a compartment for a handgun and ammunition. While people may not board a plane with arms, they do carry weapons on the streets and in nonboarding areas of airports.

Passport Caution

Always protect your passport. United States passports go at a high premium on the global black market. Never place passports, tickets, or money in a shirt pocket unless you are wearing a jacket; even then you run the risk of losing them to a professional pickpocket.

Go to an upscale luggage store and ask to see the latest means of protecting your money. New types of wallets and purses are being designed constantly to meet the needs of travelers.

Methods of keeping money secure will vary with individuals. Just make sure you find a method that works for you and with which you can be comfortable.

Wherever you choose to carry your passport and cash, don't keep patting or reaching for the pocket to check on it. That action clearly points to your money. Protection of yourself and your possessions will vary with the location. Never place the temptation of unguarded money or valuables in front of others, including team members. Leave expensive jewelry and unnecessary credit cards at home.

Security of Baggage

Baggage theft and pilfering have always been predictable problems in foreign airports. They are now serious problems in North American airports as well. Put identity tags on all baggage, including carry-on. For security purposes, use a business address or use tags which have a flap that covers your address. Also put full identification *inside* each piece of baggage.

Be sure to remove all old airport routing tags.

Passengers often forget to put identification on carry-on items which they plan to keep at arm's reach. If those items are taken from you in the boarding area, and they have no identification tags, they are easy targets for unscrupulous baggage handlers.

Many luggage keys are interchangeable, so professional baggage thieves have keys to almost everyone's luggage. Locked luggage will slow down thieves, but not stop them. One night I watched baggage handlers unload an airliner in Haiti. They repeatedly dropped a hardsided vanity case, apparently hoping for it to open. A strap often secures hardsided luggage and slows down thieves. Don't be paranoid about loss of luggage or theft, but do keep one rule in mind. Never place any item in your checked baggage that you can't afford to lose. This includes items of sentimental value. If you can't stand to lose it, put it in your carry-on or leave it at home.

If you are taking boxes that are tied and strapped, slip a small pair of scissors or a small utility knife into a side pocket of a *checked* suitcase. You'll need a cutting instrument if customs officials want the boxes opened. Have extra tape and cord handy to reseal the boxes before continuing your trip.

Cut the Chances of Lost Luggage

Early check-in is the best way to assure that your baggage arrives on the same plane as you do. If you check in late, especially during heavy travel seasons, your luggage may be put on the next plane or held until a flight leaves with a lighter passenger load.

The team that arrived on the field in swim attire flew during the Christmas holidays and stayed at the beach until the last minute before catching their flight. Their luggage arrived four days later, when passenger traffic had slacked off.

Take a Number

Before you leave your home, decide how you will protect your money and baggage from theft. The next phase of security begins as you load the car. Don't depend on a mate or a leader to protect your belongings. The first thing to do is "find your number." Your number is the number of items for which you are responsible. If it is only a backpack, your number is one. If it is a purse, a carry-on, an umbrella, and one checked suitcase, your number is four. If traveling as a couple, decide who will be responsible for which items. Every time you change locations or your luggage is shifted, count off the items for which you are responsible. Always know where you last saw all the items for which you are accountable. Start counting when your luggage goes into a vehicle outside your home. Keep counting until your belongings arrive back home. This is not a paranoid fear of theft, but a responsible accounting for your belongings at all times.

Safety Tips for Cities and Crime Corridors

If connecting flights require you to stay overnight in a major city, do not go wandering around at night unless you are well acquainted with the city. In the motel, follow safety procedures that wise travelers practice in any part of the world.

- Do not reveal your room number or future plans to strangers.
- Lock all door locks when in the motel or hotel room.
- Don't respond to random knocks without knowing who it is.
- Don't permit repairmen or other hotel employees in room without first checking with hotel management.

In 1972, when my husband, daughter, and I flew home from Bolivia, we had to stay all night in Miami. That night, we took a taxi to a nearby motel, but the next morning we walked to the airport. Times have changed. Be aware of your surroundings.

Many international flights originate in a major metropolitan area *and* in a major crime area. Robberies of tourists are not spur-of-the-moment crimes. These acts are committed by predators who cruise the area around airports looking for unsuspecting victims. No one can be completely protected from these criminals, but observance of a few safety tips will sharply reduce the possibility of an attack.

In nature, three things help protect animals: alertness, camouflage, and staying with the group. A lion does not attack a gazelle that is constantly aware of unusual movements or scents. However, a lion will attack a straggler unaware of its surroundings. In the same way, criminals can spot tourists who are following their curiosity and not paying attention to their surroundings. There is no substitute for alertness. Just as subconsciously you remember the number that represents your belongings, stay alert to all that surrounds you. Be aware of who is next to you, who has fallen in step with you, who is brushing against you, and who is staying close to you in traffic. Don't walk down stairwells, isolated corridors, or drive down side streets. Stay with the crowds and the traffic. Again, this isn't a paranoid, expecting-to-be-robbed attitude. It is the acceptance of personal responsibility for your own safety.

In the danger corridor around airports you can reduce your chances of being quickly identified as a tourist by following these suggestions.

- Choose a rental car that does not bear a rental insignia. Criminals target rental cars because they believe the driver will be carrying cash.
- Before traveling to an airport in an unfamiliar city, take time to prepare. Buy a city map. Fold the map so that the entire route is visible. You may want to mark the route with a transparent, bright, marker. Write down each change in the route on a sheet of paper. If you are driving alone, write each connection in large enough letters that you can read it while driving.
- Keep the map handy, but folded small and unobtrusive.
- If you have passengers, designate one as navigator and have that person read off approaching exits, mileage to turnoffs, and proper lanes for the exits.
- Do not hang clothes in car.
- Put luggage out of sight. Cover baggage that won't fit in the trunk.
- Put cameras out of sight.
- Never put a purse or attaché case on your lap or in the seat beside you. Put them in the trunk or on the floor. A purse or

attaché case in view is an invitation for criminals to smash a window and steal the bag while you're stopped at an intersection.

- Have a full tank of gas.
- Lock all doors and keep the windows up.
- Avoid the curb lane as much as possible.
- Don't resist muggers, especially in the US, as they are often armed and don't mind killing.
- Drive with the flow of traffic. Even if your license tags say Wisconsin and you're driving for the first time in Los Angeles, act as if you know exactly where you are going. If you miss your exit, drive as if that is exactly what you wanted to do. Do not drive slowly, braking at every street, trying to read street signs.
- Do not ask people along the street or in traffic for directions. Go to the nearest service station or chain restaurant and park. Ask directions inside, or figure out your location on the map and the route back to the main thoroughfare. While parked, keep alert to your surroundings.
- In high-crime areas, seek to blend. Be a tourist in resort areas, theme parks, or other low-crime areas. In high-crime areas, passengers should avoid leaning forward, gawking, or pointing. Keep a sharp lookout for problems, but don't gawk at the people on the street. Act as if you've gone through the neighborhood so many times that it's boring.
- If someone rear-ends your car or points to a problem with the car, *do not get out of the car.* Turn on emergency flashers and drive to the nearest, well-lighted service station or restaurant. Call 911 or the local police.

Your chances of becoming a tourist victim are remote, but take responsibility for your own safety.

Street Wisdom

- Never go out alone; go with a friend. Tell the leader where you are going and when you expect to return.
- If you go out in the neighborhood, always carry identification and information about the mission project: contact person, phone number, and location.

- Don't carry large amounts of cash. Carrying a purse under your arm or wearing a money belt won't stop armed robbers. Carry what you need for a meal and bus fare in a pocket. Give up your money rather than your life.
- Use charge cards or get small amounts of cash with an ATM card. Make withdrawals during the day and in a well-lighted and protected place like a supermarket or mall.
- Go easy on direct eye contact with people on the street. On the streets of your small hometown you may look everyone in the eye and greet them. In the city, unless you have some direct dealings with a person, avoid penetrating gazes. If you see an unusual person or situation, avoid staring.
- Stay calm in tough situations.

On Location

- Do not subject anyone to unnecessary temptation. Wherever you work or stay, never leave cameras, purses, tape players, or any item of value unattended.
- Don't flash wads of money.
- Obey the team leader's instructions. On the foreign field, volunteers are taught to trust the missionary's perception of danger and to immediately respond to any instructions. In inner-city situations, respond immediately to instructions from leaders. Ask questions later.
- Don't go off on a project of your own. Stay with the team. Warnings against doing something else may be given for reasons of which you will not be aware.
- Guard equipment, especially electronic equipment. In downtown Lake Worth, Florida, we lost an entire collection of background tapes while transferring audiovisual equipment from a van to the church.
- Women should especially be careful with purses, even in church services. Keep purses on your lap. Do not put the purse beside you on the seat because when you stand to sing or pray, you will probably leave the purse on the seat. There, it can easily be pilfered.

- Don't give out your address if no one is at your home.
- When leaving the project site, let the team leader know where you are going and when you expect to return. Always go with a friend.

CHAPTER 13

Travel Day

Arrive Early

Plan to arrive two hours in advance of departure. Lines for international flights move more slowly because of documentation and excess baggage.

If you are making connections with a team which comes from a different locale, go to the prearranged location first. If you do not find the team members, ask the ticket agent if other members have checked in. Check with the agent to make sure that you do have the correct date and location, and that the team is expected to arrive. If the team hasn't arrived 45 minutes before departure, call the mission tour agency for instructions. They may instruct you to board the flight alone or to wait until the team arrives.

If you miss a flight or connection with team members, and the team has already gone ahead, call the US mission tour agency for instructions.

Group Check-in

When team members are coming from a single church or have traveled to the airport together, a team leader may be able to check the entire team in at one time. If so, give the leader your passport and ticket. During check-in time stay with the group. Don't wander away to explore, get coffee, or go to the rest room. You may be called to the ticket desk to verify identification or clarify details. Any time you leave the group, be sure to tell someone where you are going, because the team leader may need to reach you with some last-minute instruction.

The team leader may give each member an identifying badge and team luggage tags. (These tags do not take the place of personal luggage identification tags.) If the tour organization does not supply tags, the team leader may tie pieces of yarn or tape on the checked luggage for fast and easy identification in baggage claim.

When your airline ticket is returned to you, either by an agent or a team leader, make sure that you get your passport. *Check your ticket* to make sure the correct coupon was pulled. We had to return to one airport and wait while an agent sifted through wastebaskets looking for a coupon which was pulled in error.

Airport Safety

1. Never leave a bag unattended—even for a few minutes.
2. Never carry packages through a security checkpoint for someone you have just met, even if it's a helpless mother with toddlers or an elderly gentleman with a walker. One kind Haitian woman who helped a feeble woman with a package is now serving a prison sentence for drug possession.
3. Do not touch an unattended bag. If you listen to the public address system in major airports, you will hear these warnings issued repeatedly. Leave unattended bags and cameras alone. Finders are not keepers. Some major airports have conducted sting operations. Travelers who picked up items and did not take them to lost and found promptly were arrested.

Saying Good-bye

Before boarding, leave any unnecessary coats with friends at the boarding gate. Be sure to leave keys if someone is driving your car

---

X-ray Inspections

According to the National Association of Photographic Manufacturers, avoid X-ray inspection of photograph films faster than ISO (ASA) 400. The effect on lower speed film, video tapes, and computer disks is negligible. **Hand carry insulin through security checks.** Repeated or prolonged exposure to X-ray will damage insulin.

Travel Comfort

Women—Don't wear high heels on travel day. In the airport, you may have to walk long distances at a fast pace. Wear a dress flat or comfortable low heel.

Air-conditioning—If you get cold on planes, take a jacket or sweater. Don't wear heavy clothing, especially if you are going to the tropics. Many airports are not air-conditioned and you'll be miserable in immigration and customs lines.

Cologne/Perfume—Consider fellow passengers. Go easy on cologne and perfume.

---

home. In all the excitement, team members often forget basic arrangements. When you say good-bye, don't forget you are coming back. If friends are picking you up at the airport in which you clear customs, tell them to meet you in the *customs waiting area*. Warn them that delays of an hour or more are common when several international planes arrive at the same time.

Travel Etiquette

Let your surroundings set the tone of your behavior on the plane. Years ago, we flew the US-Guatemala route several times. Sometimes we flew Pan Am and other times a Guatemalan airline. Aboard Pan Am planes, passengers pulled the white shades against the sun and read compactly folded *Wall Street Journals* as the plane gently lifted into the sky. The plane was immaculate with only the lingering odor of stale tobacco. Passengers ordered drinks from the stewardess with a nod of the head and only left their seats to use the rest room.

On the Guatemalan plane, an orange one that everyone called the "flying papaya," the fold-down trays were unwiped, the floor unvacuumed, and the cabin smelled of Guatemalan textiles. As soon as the plane roared into the sky, it banked sharply allowing passengers to see Miami. While we hung sideways, seat belts clanked open and people on the high side of the plane rushed to the lower side to see the view. Everyone talked excitedly about the sights. No one on those flights read a paper, slept, or stayed seated.

Take your cue about plane etiquette from fellow passengers. If you end up on a flight with excited tourists traveling to Rio, then joking across the aisle to a fellow team member is in order. If, however, the passengers seem aloof, buried in books, or trying to sleep, keep your conversation quiet and unobtrusive.

To appear as a seasoned international traveler:

- Be sensitive to your seat mates. Don't push conversation.
- Be careful about what you tell a stranger. Do not reveal too much of future plans, especially if you are traveling alone, or plan to stay in public accommodations.
- Do not give your name and home address to strangers, especially if your home is unattended while you are away. If you want to keep in touch with someone you meet on the plane, give your church address, not your home address. There are always exceptions. On one flight I exchanged addresses with a veteran missionary from another organization. As a rule, though, do not give out your address to someone you just met.
- Make sure you are not creating problems for the flight crew or fellow passengers. On one return trip, I did everything I could to disassociate myself with a team I accompanied. While hostesses struggled with carts in the narrow aisles, team members asked for special favors, made trips to the rest room, and lounged in the aisles recounting their adventures. They told their stories in a loud boisterous manner, in order to witness to everyone in surrounding seats. Their *witness* was poor, to say the least.
- Be gracious and friendly, but mix friendliness with worldly wisdom.

Airline Safety

Staying healthy and avoiding accidents begin on the plane. Wearing a seat belt is a must for safe automobile travel in any country. Keeping your seat belt fastened *at all times* is also a must for safe air travel. Nearly all in-flight injuries could be prevented if seat belts were kept fastened. Even on clear days planes may pass through invisible pockets of turbulence that cause abrupt changes in altitude. After takeoff, you may loosen a seat belt, but always keep it fastened.

Special Tips for Transcontinental Flights

1. Proper sitting helps minimize aches and pains, sore backs, and swollen feet. Keep your seat upright or slightly tilted backward, put a firm pillow or blanket in the small of your back, and fasten the seat belt tightly around your hips.
2. Keep the back of your thighs off the seat by slightly elevating your feet. If necessary, rest your feet on a briefcase, bag, or blanket. Keep legs uncrossed. Crossing your legs shifts body weight to your lower back, causing pain and interfering with blood circulation to your legs.
3. Remove objects from your back pocket. Prolonged sitting on a bulky wallet, for example, exerts pressure on the sciatic nerve, causing pain in your lower back and legs.
4. Occasionally walk about for exercise.
5. Wear shoes with laces. Remove them once you are airborne and exercise your feet frequently by moving your toes. Shoes with laces are easier to put back on if feet swell.
6. Take only essential medications.
7. Wear contact lenses only if necessary.
8. Avoid greasy foods and foods that promote gas.
9. Carry a sweater or jacket. The airplane cabin may get chilly.
10. Use saline eyedrops every few hours.[1]

If your flight is on a world-class airline the food will probably be as safe as airline food gets. If the flight is on a smaller airline departing from a well-developed nation, it will probably be safe. If the food is being loaded from an underdeveloped nation, or a developing nation, avoid salads, water, ice cubes, and cold meats. Hot, well-cooked food, breads, crackers, or peelable fruits are considered safe on any flight. If in doubt, don't eat it. Get a granola bar out of your carry-on.

Be sure to drink plenty of fluids to counteract dehydration from low cabin humidity.

Immigration Forms

On the plane, you will usually be given immigration forms which will request name, address, purpose of visit, name and address of hotel or person with whom you will be staying, port of embarkation, and airline carrier. On the purpose-of-visit line, mark *pleasure* or *tourist*. Business means that you are there to work and conduct business for profit. *Other* is for students and those staying for extended periods of time. *Never put missionary.* You are entering the country as a tourist and are there on pleasure.

Before exiting the plane get your document pouch in order. Make sure you have tickets, passport, visa, immigration form, name and address of hotel or person with whom you'll be staying, and tip money handy. You may need to show your return ticket in immigration to prove that you plan to return home.

As incredible as it may seem, one team member placed his return ticket in the flap of the plane seat in front of him. He forgot about his ticket until he arrived at the guest house and the missionary collected the return tickets for safekeeping.

On one occasion, I saw a truckload of waving, singing, yelling volunteers driving toward the headquarters of another mission organization. As they passed, papers blew out of the truck. Curious, I picked up the papers—including someone's return airline ticket. **Before leaving the plane,** make sure all documents are safely tucked into your document pouch and the document pouch is in a secure but easy-to-reach place.

CHAPTER 14

Arrival

Welcoming Parties

Musicians may greet you. You don't have to tip but you may. Everyone around you will be moving quickly toward immigration, so don't hold up traffic by rummaging for change. Toss in some of your handy tip money, and keep on moving.

Your first stop will be immigration. Don't worry about missing it. Signs will direct you. Your only entrance to the rest of the airport will be through immigration.

Your servant attitude needs to be evident in the airport. If lines are long and you are hot and thirsty, don't talk about the way it is back home. If people crowd ahead of you in line, watch your attitude.

The concept of single-file lines with a two-foot space between people is alien to some cultures. In some countries, people simply do not line up, they crowd to a ticket window or through a gate. If you are in a situation where people cut in and take up the space between you and the person ahead of you, do not get upset. Move up until your body is nearly touching the person ahead, then keep shuffling forward.

Immigration

At immigration have in hand your passport, your visa, the immigration form which you filled out on the plane, and your return ticket.

Pay special attention to all the signs and stay behind designated lines until motioned to enter the checkpoint. Each person goes through immigration alone. Don't try to go through with a spouse. Don't be nervous about immigration and customs. Answer questions truthfully. Your luggage won't be with you at this time so there may not be any questions about items you're carrying.

As a rule, immigration officials say very little. They may ask where you·are staying or why you are there. The less you say, the better off you'll be. Be courteous. Answer questions.

Do not elaborate and try to evangelize and win over officials with your friendliness. This is not the time to say, "Bless God, I'm Reverend Jimmy Johnson and I've come to preach the gospel."

Even if you appear on TV weekly or have built multimillion dollar shopping malls or do open-heart surgery, pass through the gate of immigration as a servant. Keep in mind that people in these countries are sensitive about North Americans taking jobs from them and about the superior attitudes of North Americans.

If questioned further, which is rare, tell the official where you are going and the name of the mission organization. In your own words, say that you've come to visit the country and give the mission organization a helping hand. Don't try to impress anyone with your importance. Never say you are coming as a missionary. Missionaries are barred from some countries; in other countries they must have a permanent resident visa, which requires wading through months of red tape.

Your best witness in immigration is simply responding to the questions in a gracious way that focuses on the attractions of that country rather than your gifts of expertise or service to that country.

If you don't understand the officer due to an accent, shake your head that you don't understand. If it is important, they will find someone to interpret. Again, problems in immigration are rare if you have a passport.

Baggage Pickup

You will probably have a few minutes between clearing immigration and picking up baggage. Use that time to put tickets, visas, and passports in a safe but easy-to-reach place. **Do not throw away any papers.** One team member threw away her visa after she passed through immigration. Wait until you get home to throw away papers.

Get keys to luggage and tip money handy. Ask the team leader what arrangements have been made to handle baggage after clearing customs.

If you are traveling in a group, work with the team in retrieving baggage. Two or three people can watch the pile of carry-on luggage; two or three can wait by the carousel to pull off luggage; and two or three can carry luggage to the guarded pile.

As you are waiting, be careful of comments, especially in the presence of military personnel. Soldiers in other countries are often trained by English-speaking Americans. Many words in English are similar in other languages.

In a country that was changing presidents every six months, and whose airport was manned by machine gun-toting soldiers, a Michigan volunteer called loudly to a team member in the next customs lane, "What did you tell them was our reason for being here? Missionary? Or mercenary?" When you travel to another culture, you'll think of many hilarious one-liners, but save them for an appropriate time. Also, don't be surprised to find that airports in undeveloped countries are guarded by soldiers with machine guns. This is not uncommon.

If luggage for the team was checked in together, the team leader will have all the baggage claim tickets. Do not take your bags through customs until all pieces of luggage have been collected. If one piece is missing, the leader will need to check all the claim tickets against all pieces of baggage in order to determine the claim number of the missing baggage. Trying to match the numbers after the bags have been loaded into vans or taxis is very difficult. Once all bags are accounted for, proceed with your bags through customs.

Customs

Couples may work together going through customs. Unlock suitcases, undo straps, have knife handy to cut string or tape on boxes. Put everything, including purses and document pouches on the counter or conveyor belt. Do not open anything until requested.

They may have you open every bag, only one bag, or no bags. Sometimes, if the officials are familiar with the mission organization, they will wave a team through without opening a bag. Other times, they will pull everything out and leave you trying to stuff it all back in the suitcase. On one occasion, the officer simply asked for the purse I had forgotten to remove from my shoulder.

Another time, I followed a team member through customs who regularly visited the mission field. This woman had placed coloring books and crayons on the top of her clothes. As the agent lifted the edges of clothes, she caressed the books, smiled and said, "For your children? You may have for your children." He had no problem understanding her English.

I had just come in from a medical leave in the States and had brought our daughter a couple of music tapes. The customs official picked up one of the tapes and looked me in the eye. I simply returned his gaze. He moved on through the clothing, picked up another tape and held it until I looked up. I still just returned his gaze. He picked up the first tape again and held it and looked at me. "For *my* daughter," I said.

The visiting team member was able to make her entry through customs easier, but she set up problems for team members and missionaries who followed her.

If customs officials question any item you have, simply reply *for personal use* or *for a friend*. Do not give any items away. If an agent shows a desire for something, ignore the gesture. If an item is seized by customs, the missionary will be able to get it released or know the correct amount of duty to be paid. Don't show the receipts for purchases unless specifically requested to do so. Team members seldom have problems in customs, but please, don't be the cause of future problems.

Outside the Airport

The most chaotic and frightening time of a tour usually occurs when you step outside the airport. In many foreign airports, vendors, beggars, and children may surround you. Children will literally start peeling your luggage from your hands in order to earn a few coins.

On a well-organized tour, a missionary or the team leader will handle your baggage. They will often have selected porters which they use on a regular basis. If you are on an all-inclusive trip, your tips will be handled by the team leader or missionary.

Before you exit a foreign airport, know how the tour leaders have arranged for handling your luggage. If no arrangements have been made, decide whether you can manage your baggage alone in a crowded situation.

If you know that you will need help, follow these guidelines.
1. Have tip money (in small bills and coins) in hand.
2. Look for uniformed or badged baggage porters inside the airport.
3. If none are available inside, look for uniformed or badged baggage porters just outside the door.
4. If there are no uniformed porters available, either inside or outside, you'll need to choose a porter from the mob outside. Take a minute to quickly scan the crowd. Don't let pity entice you to give your luggage to begging children. Your belongings may go in three different directions. Quickly look for a teenager or an adult. Ask him to carry your luggage. He may give the children orders to pick up your luggage, but he will take charge of the children. When you pay, pay only the adult, but use small bills and coins so that he can pay the children. When the children demand pay, point to the person to whom you gave the money. **Never give a porter your bag with document pouch, money, or valuables.** Keep that bag in your own hands.

If the next leg of your trip is in a missionary vehicle, you can relax a little more about the safety of your luggage. If you are going to be traveling several hours, however, you'll probably want to keep your carry-on within arm's reach so that you can grab one of your snacks.

CHAPTER 15

Safe Choices

Laws of the Land

One visitor in Washington, D.C., inquired at a visitor's bureau, "As a tourist, am I immune to the traffic laws, stoplights, and things like that?" We laugh, but many North Americans traveling abroad assume they are exempt from foreign laws. In foreign countries, you are subject to all laws of that nation. Many foreign laws are stricter than US laws. If you are arrested, the missionary or team leader will contact the nearest consulate, but don't expect the marines to come to your rescue. Your US and Canadian constitutional rights do not travel with you. You will be held, arraigned, tried, and sentenced according to the laws of that nation, not the laws of the United States or Canada.

To avoid breaking laws, always conduct yourself as a law-abiding North American. Pay attention to briefings. The team leader or missionary should inform you about any unusual laws.

As a rule, unusual laws or regulations will usually fall into one of these categories: money exchange; traffic patterns and regulations; standards for public dress; photography; political expression; religious activities; contraband substances; and antiquities.

Driving in Foreign Countries

Most personal injuries and tangles with law enforcement in foreign countries are due to traffic accidents. **Don't drive unless absolutely necessary.** Traffic patterns and traffic laws differ from nation to nation. If you are driving and are involved in an accident, you may have to stay in the country several months until trial. Don't let anyone pressure you into driving unless you are comfortable with the situation. Most mission tour organizations will provide drivers.

Unwritten Laws of the Land

Survival in an emergency situation often means knowledge of and obedience to the *unwritten* laws of the land.

While our family was traveling through a tranquil, seemingly unpopulated area of Haiti, a woman ran across the road in front of our truck. We could not avoid hitting her. We stopped, grabbed our first-aid kit, and went to assist her. She appeared to have only minor scrapes and bruises, but out of nowhere people began to gather. The tone of the people did not sound friendly. To make a long story short, we barely escaped with our lives.

When we reported the incident to officials in the city, we were told, "In rural areas, **never, ever,** stop at the scene of an accident. The people out there have their own laws and ways of meting out justice. **Never stop.** Always go to the nearest police station. Report the accident, then return with police protection to the scene."

In the event of an accident or emergency, volunteers should be in complete subjection to the missionary. The missionary may not have time to explain why some things are done a certain way. Trust the missionary's judgment and obey immediately. Insistence on doing what you think is right might clear your conscience, but it could jeopardize the lives of the entire team. In a crisis, simply obey the missionary and sort out the moral implications later.

Pedestrians

In most countries, pedestrians **do not** have the right of way.

Passports

Guard your passport. Overseas, a US passport is more precious than gold. Sometimes the missionary or team leader will collect passports for safekeeping. If you don't need to carry your passport, put it in a safe place and carry a photocopy of the ID page.

Pay Close Attention to Briefings

Once you arrive and get settled into your room, the team leader or missionary will probably hold an on-site briefing session. Take your notebook and pen to this briefing session. You'll be given a lot of information regarding house rules, schedules, cultural do's and don'ts, and plans for the next days. Don't try to remember it all, take notes. Also, the first night will be hectic. Wait until the next day to give the missionary receipts for items you've purchased by request.

Security: Self

1. Always carry identification.
2. Always let someone on the team know where you are going and when you expect to return.
3. Check with the missionary or team leader before going out alone. It's always better to have a companion.
4. In a city, follow the safety rules you would heed in any large North American city.
5. If you are in a politically sensitive country, be careful what you write in journals, say in public, and say on the phone. In some countries, many international calls are monitored by government officials. Personally, you will probably encounter no problem, but the mission organization may be placed under surveillance. If you have any negative observations about politics or national religions, save your comments until you return home.

Security: Belongings

Many people in developing nations live by the philosophy of *You have so much, you won't miss this,* or *If you don't have an item securely in your possession, you don't want it.*

We, of course, have a different philosophy. We believe *I need everything that I have,* and *What is mine is mine, unless I give it to you.*

Taking personal responsibility for the security of your possessions does not end when you unpack at a motel or mission's guest house, or when you arrive at a church. If you follow a few guidelines, however, you can keep your belongings safe.

1. If the missionary has a safe, put extra money, passports, tickets, etc., in the safe.
2. Missionaries live by the rule, *Do not subject employees to unnecessary temptation.* Whether in a mission guest house or a four-star motel, take time to put your belongings away before you leave your room for the day. Spread a towel or T-shirt over your belongings in drawers or suitcases, so that nothing of value is visible at first sight. You may leave toiletries out because they can be replaced easily; but put away expensive perfumes or aftershaves.
3. During church services, women should keep purses on their laps. Large bags can be placed between the feet on the floor. Do not put the purse beside you on the seat because when you stand for prayer, you will probably leave the purse on the seat where it can easily be pilfered when all eyes are closed. In the English-speaking church in Haiti, several missionaries lost a lot of cash because they got careless about *watching and praying.*
4. On-site security. Whether you sight-see, conduct a Vacation Bible School, or build a clinic, you will probably carry a daily tote bag with a little cash, camera, snacks, etc. The team leader or missionary will tell you where to place tote bags for safekeeping. The safe place may be a locked vehicle, a storage shed, or a church member's house. As long as you follow the missionary or team leader's instructions you can relax about the safety of your tote bag.
5. Equipment security. Construction, music, and drama teams often have problems with equipment security. Since foreign visitors always attract a lot of attention in a community, construction

sites and stages swarm with curious observers—both Christian and non-Christian. While volunteers are busy making new friends, hammers, trowels, chalk boxes, music tapes, videos, and microphones suddenly develop legs and walk away.

6. Security around children. During a nine-month project in Guatemala, members of our volunteer camp lost everything from peanut butter from the table to jeans from the clothesline. For weeks, the camp bookkeeper told me to keep my daughter's two playmates out of the camp buildings because they were stealing from us. I refused to believe the four-year-old boy and seven-year-old girl were guilty, until the day the shower house was raided. That morning, no one in camp had a toothbrush, toothpaste, razor, deodorant, or soap. We all had to go to town and buy toiletries. Conveniently, the father of our daughter's playmates had just set up a booth downtown. He was selling slightly-used razors, soap, deodorant, toothpaste, and toothbrushes. Protect children from temptation. Don't open your tote bag and show them all the wonders you've brought from your country. Keep tools, cameras, and tote bags out of the reach of children. Do not entertain children in the storage areas where supplies and equipment are stored.

Construction Teams

Never leave a tool lying around. If you leave the job site for a break, take your tools with you. When you finish with a tool, place it in the storage area. Guard mission equipment as if it were your own. On the field, tools are often hard to find and very expensive.

Music or Drama Teams

Take extra measures to keep cassette tapes, videos, electronic equipment, puppets, and stage props safe. If background tapes are essential for an evangelism program, put duplicate copies in a place other than where you usually store the tapes. Don't leave puppets lying around. Put them out of sight when not in use. When loading and unloading electronic equipment, post two security guards, one at the vehicle and one at the setup area.

Money Exchange

As a rule you will exchange money in one of the following places:
- North American airport
- Foreign airport
- Bank
- Mission headquarters

Some countries have strict rules about money exchange. You may even be expelled for using North American currency. Some require strict accounting of all cash you bring in, receipts for all exchanges, and a total of money you take out. To be on the safe side, keep all receipts for money exchanges.

In some countries the government says all purchases must be in local dollars, but no one is prosecuted for using or accepting American dollars. Check with the team leader or missionary.

Before leaving a North American airport, you may want to exchange $50 to $100 at the currency exchange, especially if you are going to take a taxi when you arrive in the foreign country. If you don't have time, or the exchange is closed, you'll have opportunity to exchange money later.

At your destination your team leader or the missionary should tell you where to exchange money. If the missionary offers to handle the exchange, let him or her do so. In many countries, missionaries can sell US dollars to merchants who need them to buy US goods. In return the missionary will receive a small premium based on the current exchange rate.

Wherever you exchange money, exchange all the money you need to exchange at one time. It's a waste of time and an inconvenience to make extra trips to the bank, or have the missionary open the safe and conduct exchange transactions. You can always trade back unused currency before departure.

Never change money on the streets. It's usually illegal. Furthermore, you may get shortchanged, receive counterfeit bills, or be a victim of a money switch scam.

CHAPTER 16

Healthy Choices

Drink

Water will be unsafe, safe, or purified. Never drink *unsafe* water, eat ice made from it, or use it to brush your teeth.

Drink *safe* water (ask the missionaries if the tap water is safe to drink) sparingly the first few days, especially if you are sensitive to water changes. This means take it easy on iced tea, lemonade, and other cold drinks made with water and served with ice cubes. Drink more hot drinks, juice, bottled water, and sodas.

If the water is *purified* (boiled, bottled, or run through a purification system), you shouldn't have any trouble drinking all you want.

Healthy Food Choices in Developing Nations

In developing nations, the food supply is contaminated due to a lack of refrigeration, lack of pasteurization processes, lack of food-handling regulations, and the use of human excrement as fertilizer. The locals seem to develop some resistance to food-related illnesses, but a tourist who is used to relatively pure food may fall victim to dysentery or food poisoning. To stay healthy, keep the method of preparation in mind when making food choices.

- **Food prepared by team members** is safe if basic rules for food handling are observed: wash hands before touching food; keep cold foods cold; keep hot foods hot. If you purchase food locally, buy fruits and vegetables that can be peeled. Avoid lettuce unless you know how to properly disinfect it. Avoid fresh meat and seafood unless you know it has been refrigerated. Use canned meat. Avoid fresh dairy products. Check with the missionary if in doubt.
- **Food prepared by mission guest house staff,** or by local cooks which the team leader or missionary has chosen, should be safe. Usually, you can eat salads because they have been properly disinfected.
- **Food prepared in restaurants** may have some unsafe items. Avoid: Uncooked meat, raw or lightly-cooked shellfish, salads, parsley, unpeelable fruits such as berries and grapes, and most milk products. Uncooked fish may contain parasites and is especially dangerous in areas where cholera is prevalent.
- Avoid: Food buffets, food which has been handled a lot, or food which has been sitting out. Two days after Fred arrived in Guatemala, he went to an outdoor buffet, at one of Antigua's finest restaurants. He ate several plates of fresh fruit. Two days later he had to fly home because unrelenting vomiting, cramps, and diarrhea had caused an ulcer to start bleeding. Avoid buffets and don't overindulge on any one food, even fruit.
- Best choices: Fully-cooked food served hot; fresh breads; fruits that you peel—(bananas, oranges, apples, mangos, coconuts, etc.); bottled water; bottled drinks; or hot drinks such as coffee. Remember ice is often made from impure water.
- Food prepared on the street is the most dangerous. The food at roadside stands looks good and smells scrumptious. Be

advised though that drinks and icy slushes are usually made with contaminated water. Flyblown meat is fried in rancid oil. Mayonnaise is never refrigerated. Dishes and silverware are sloshed through greasy cold water. If you want to try local delicacies, eat at a better restaurant or buy packaged foods from a supermarket. The missionary or team leader can suggest safe, local food items.

Emergency Rehydration

Emergency rehydration for adults: Four teaspoons of sugar (or honey); one-half teaspoon of salt; one quart of pure water.

Food Police

In some situations, even in the home of the missionary or local, you may feel that the food is unsafe. Either graciously decline the food, or take a small portion and spread it around on your plate so that it isn't so obvious that you didn't eat it. Don't announce to the group that they are going to get food poisoning if they eat it.

Seafood

Eating seafood is an individual choice. In the tropics, however, you will run a slight risk of ciguatera or *barracuda* toxic poisoning, which affects the central nervous system. The poison, found in fish that feed on coral reefs, is odorless, colorless, and cannot be cooked away. It is not caused by improper handling or preparation, but accumulates in fish. The fish do not metabolize it, humans do.

In most cases, people experience vomiting and diarrhea and very few aftereffects. A few people have serious side effects. Bizarre symptoms which may develop several days later include: reversal of sensitivity to heat and cold; stiffness in muscles; vision disturbances; temporary blindness; a debilitating malaise; and in some cases, coma.

Sanitation

Don't carry a can of disinfectant spray with you, but do pay attention to the basic rules of hygiene which you learned in elementary school. Always wash your hands before eating. Always wash hands after using the toilet.

To further reduce risk of disease, keep nails short and don't dig in the dirt with bare hands—wear gloves.

Keep your shoes on as much as possible, especially if you're in an area with little or no public sanitation service. If you're staying in a guest house, keep your shoes on in the common area where there is a lot of foot traffic from the outside.

Beaches

In cities, untreated sewage often flows into the sea. In rural areas, the beach serves as a community latrine. In developing nations, don't sit on the sand in a bathing suit. Some team members have come home with severe cases of ringworm. Always sit on a towel or beach chair.

Consult locals or missionaries before swimming in unguarded areas. Currents and undertows can pull you out to sea. If you get caught in an undertow, don't try to swim against it. Relax and go with the tow. In time it will dissipate and you can swim back to the beach.

In coral reef areas, wear old sneakers or water boots to avoid cuts on sharp coral. Avoid brushing against coral, which will destroy reefs and may give you nasty cuts. Never take live coral.

Before swimming or wading in fresh water (especially in Africa) consult the team leader or missionary. Some fresh water rivers and lakes contain snails that transmit schistosomiasis, a serious illness. You can also contract cholera by swimming in contaminated water.

HIV Virus

Am I at risk for HIV? Everyone is at risk for contracting the HIV virus. AIDS is a world disease. The same precautions must be observed in all countries. Besides the religious prohibitions of illegal drug use and sex outside of marriage, mission team members should:

1. Avoid injections and sutures unless you have either seen the items removed from a sterile pack or provided sterile equipment. In many countries, doctors do not have the luxury of

opening packets of sterile needles or sutures. A packet of butterfly closures, sterile needles, syringes and a stitch kit should accompany a team. Any doctor in the area can then use these sterile supplies to treat team members. Butterfly closures can be used to close some wounds thus avoiding stitches.

2. Cleanse and cover any wound immediately. Prevent wounds by wearing work gloves on construction projects.

3. Do not be afraid to touch children, even though they invariably have open cuts and abrasions. Protect yourself by making sure your scratches and open wounds are covered.

4. **Do not touch anyone's blood unless you are protected.** If someone is injured, even a team member, try to avoid unprotected contact with his or her blood.

5. Avoid blood transfusions. Opt for medical evacuation rather than a blood transfusion. Getting HIV virus through blood transfusion is a very real possibility in other countries. In a life-or-death emergency, the missionary will probably call on the network of blood donors in the missionary community. The blood is not screened for HIV, but the possibility of the virus is lower because of the low-risk lifestyle of missionaries. There is no guarantee, however, that this blood source is safe. **Do not use blood from a foreign blood bank unless you are sure that blood has been properly screened.** Take a chance on a team member or missionary rather than an uncertain public blood supply.

Injury

Occasionally, a team member breaks a bone or suffers some serious illness. Accept the missionary's decision about your medical care, particularly if the missionary feels you should return home. One young woman insisted on staying on the field after breaking a leg. The doctor, although one of the best in the area, did not have the equipment to detect a second break. The girl's refusal to go home ultimately resulted in surgeries, months of rehabilitation, and large medical bills. In the event of a serious injury or illness, you should usually return home immediately.

Contents Under Pressure

When traveling to high altitudes (over 8,000 ft.), watch when opening containers which have been sealed at a lower altitude. The contents may squirt or spray out. When descending, plastic bottles will collapse. It's a good idea to keep containers with liquids in snap-and-seal bags.

Higher Ground

If you travel in the Andes or other high mountain ranges you may suffer from altitude sickness. The symptoms include: headache, dizziness, shortness of breath, insomnia, and loss of appetite. To minimize these symptoms:

1. Take it easy the first few days. Stay active, but don't overdo.
2. Drink plenty of fluids to compensate for lower humidity and deeper, more rapid respirations.
3. Stay warm and dry.
4. Eat a diet high in carbohydrates.
5. Avoid carbonated drinks.
6. Most drugs, especially tranquilizers and sedatives, have more potency at high altitudes. Be alert to unusual reactions to medicine. Diamox is sometimes prescribed for altitude sickness, but don't take it if you have an allergy to sulfa.
7. If acute symptoms develop—breathing becomes impossible, hallucinations or bizarre behavior occurs—move to a lower altitude immediately.

More Healthy Choices

1. Don't nap under a coconut tree.
2. Don't lick stamps.[1]
3. Don't use tap water on contact lenses.

CHAPTER 17

Living in the Land

Conserve Water

"I thought going on a mission trip would make me appreciate home more," Rachel said. "I never dreamed it would happen so soon."

One of the first lessons you'll probably learn on the foreign mission field is to appreciate clean, flowing water. In developing countries, few people have constant access to running water. In cities, water flows to specific areas on set days where homeowners store the water in cisterns. During rainy season, supplemental water is collected on flat roofs and drained to the cistern. During dry seasons, water must be purchased and hauled to the cistern. Island nations especially have critical shortages of fresh water.

If the missionary or team leader brings water conservation to your attention, do take their advice seriously. This will mean *not* letting the water run while you shave, brush your teeth, or lather up in the shower. It will also mean flushing the toilet only when necessary.

Conserve Electricity

Electricity may be intermittent. Even though the quality of service in developing nations cannot approach that of developed nations, the electric bill can. Generally, in developing countries, electricity costs twice as much as in North America. Do turn out all lights and fans when you leave a room.

Accommodations

- Motel—Even though you are with a team in your own country, observe motel safety rules.
- Recreational vehicles or travel trailers—Ask ahead about parking. Will it be at the church or at a campground?
- Church facilities—Ask if you'll need to bring bedding. Will you be sleeping on the floor? If so, consider taking a 4-inch-thick piece of foam to place under your sleeping bag. If staying in church facilities, conserve on water and electricity.
- Local homes or missionary—Always be a good houseguest. Pick up and clean up after yourself. Conserve electricity and water. Respect the owners privacy. Don't snoop. Always leave the home and furnishings in the condition you found them.

Unless you're staying in a motel, you'll probably be sharing a bathroom. Be sure to take along towels, washcloths, and modest sleeping attire. In camp accommodations you'll need flip-flops for the shower. Make toilet and shower times as brief as possible when several are waiting in line. Don't hog the hot water.

Bathroom Surprises

One missionary said, "Volunteers should be prepared to encounter different toilet facilities." In better public rest rooms, attendants often hand out the toilet tissue. The attendant will expect a small coin. Pay it and complain later.

Some bathrooms, either in public or in homes, may have a small waste can near the toilet which holds used tissue. This means

Photography

Be sensitive. In some countries it may be illegal to take photographs of things like government buildings or soldiers. Check with the missionary or local leader connected to your project. While our country allows photography of almost anything or anyone, do respect the individual. Treat others as you would want to be treated. Pass up a photo opportunity to preserve a relationship.

1. Fill the frame with the photo. Get close.
2. Change your position. Don't be afraid to stoop or to climb for a different viewpoint.
3. Shoot both horizontal and vertical pictures.
4. Use the rule of thirds in shooting pictures. Don't divide a photo in half by putting the horizon in the middle. Put the point of interest a third from top or bottom, or a third from the left or right.
5. Check the background to make sure signs or posts don't appear to protrude from heads.
6. When shooting photographs in the shade or of dark-skinned people, try one shot at the correct light and one with more light.
7. Avoid backgrounds of open doors or windows, unless you want silhouettes.
8. Use telephoto lenses to get good shots without drawing attention to yourself or irritating people.
9. When doing close shots of people, establish rapport first, then ask permission.
10. Respect the wishes of those who do not want to be photographed. (Would you want someone photographing you in your worst clothes?)
11. Photograph people in action rather than posed rows. Combine people with landmarks or objects of cultural interest.
12. In tense or politically sensitive areas, do not point cameras at policemen, military officers, military installations, or government buildings. In all countries, be careful about taking pictures of accidents or public disturbances.
13. If you plan a slide show or display of photos, choose a theme and get pictures that will reflect the theme.
14. Get a team photo with yourself in it. Be sure you appear in some of the other photos also.

that **tissue should not be flushed** down the toilet because the pipes are too small. As distasteful as it may seem, do discard tissue in the receptacle, not in the toilet. This is especially important if you are staying in a local home or in mission guest accommodations.

Sometimes there are simply no toilet facilities. When teams make a rest stop, the men go to one side of the road and the women to the other side. Surprisingly, when you get into such a situation it turns out to be no big deal. It's just the way life is in those countries. Rather than feeling embarrassment, you gain a deeper understanding of how the local people really live.

Tipping

Tipping policies vary from nation to nation and even locations within a nation. In Latin America, Africa, and the Middle East you must tip if you expect to get service. If you have an aversion to tipping, lay down your rights to your own aversions and **tip.** Some North Americans have blurted out, "I work for my money. No one tips me. I'm not going to pay someone to bring me a soda." The missionaries constantly deal with the people you will be meeting. The service the missionary receives tomorrow will depend on the tips you give today. Don't overtip, because that creates problems for a next team, but do give a fair tip.

In a few countries, tipping is considered offensive. If you are going into Asia, China, Indonesia, or the South Pacific, check on the policies. Wherever you go, though, tips are usually expected in Western hotels and restaurants. Some of the all-inclusive mission tour prices include all tips.

Never hand a paltry tip to the missionary to pass on.

Observe

Don't cover your ears with headphones or bury yourself in a magazine from home. Observe. You will increase the long-term benefits of your mission tour by observing and recording your observations. You don't need to write in detail about your experiences, but do take time to *observe in detail.*

Watch out the window of the vehicle. Take a walk through the neighborhood. Buy a local newspaper; even if you can't read the language, you will probably be able to understand the advertisements and photos. If there is a store or supermarket nearby, try some of the national snacks. Stick to items produced and packaged by food companies.

Use all your senses. Load all the sights, sounds, and smells you can into your memory bank. Let the experience soak in. Then, during a break in the schedule, quickly jot down what stands out in your memory of the last hours. Keep your notes up to date. Before going to bed, or first thing the next morning, bring your journal notes up to date. The new day will be so full of events that you will forget the details of yesterday's experiences.

Session Three
Individual or Group Assignments

Language Study

1. Prepare at least one song in the language of the people you plan to visit. Even a chorus will work. The people you visit will appreciate your efforts to communicate in their language.
2. Find someone in your area who is from the country you plan to visit and who speaks the language. Ask the person to give you an insider's view of the culture. What are the taboos? Also ask for assistance in pronunciation of words, especially those in the song you plan to sing.
3. Give your personal testimony. If possible, do it through an interpreter.

Work Together to Finish Projects and Meet Needs

Are crafts cut and bagged? Do you have all the tools and equipment necessary to complete a project? What about luggage? Does anyone need to borrow a piece of luggage? Are the carrying cases for fragile equipment on hand? Who is responsible for the first-aid kit? Work together to make sure logistical details are worked out in advance.

If you plan to double up on packing, decide who will bring which items. Ask someone on the team to keep track of what each person has promised to supply or do.

Strengthen Links to the Home Church

Discuss ways to forge stronger bonds with your home church. For example: keep the regular church body informed on team plans and progress by use of bulletin inserts or two-minute mission infomercials during regular services.

Team Prayer

During this session focus prayers on:

- The particular ministry in which you'll be participating on the field. Pray about the logistical preparations. Pray for wisdom in ministry methods.

- Pray for the people to whom you'll minister. Pray that God will begin to prepare their hearts and will remove hindrances to their acceptance of the gospel.
- Pray for teammates. Pray that logistical and financial needs will be met. Pray for a spirit of unity among team members.

Assignment

Prepare the list of emergency information for your family.

If you have a new or unfamiliar camera or tape recorder, shoot a practice roll of film or record a church service. Note the distractions. Repeat the exercise and see if you can make improvements.

Write out answers to the following questions.

1. List five ways that you think the missionary family would spend recreational or free time.
2. Other than religious, list three types of books that you think you would find in a missionary's bookcase.
3. List three ways that you think missionaries would spend extra cash.
4. Be prepared to share a story about roommates (not spouses or siblings).

Use these questions during your group time to spur conversation about expectations related to missionaries and roommates.

PART FOUR

Relationships

CHAPTER 18

Teamwork

Mission Tours Are Not Vacations

When you go on vacation, you plan to abandon schedules, choose fun activities, relax, eat sumptuously, be pampered, and be entertained. You expect to return home tanned, relaxed, a few pounds heavier, and many dollars poorer.

When you go on a mission tour, you are asked to adhere to a strict schedule, participate in team activities, work (possibly harder than at home), eat what is placed before you, and serve others. You will return from the mission tour, tired, grubby looking, hungry for familiar food, and spiritually wealthier.

The benefits of a *vacation* fade as quickly as your tan. The benefits of a *mission tour* will increase with time.

Going with the proper understanding of the difference between a vacation and a mission tour will enable you to better understand the importance of teamwork.

Where's the Red Carpet?

Some host congregations may welcome teams with balloons and a songfest. Other congregations may barely acknowledge your presence. While a negative reception is rare, the prepared volunteer accepts the disappointments as well as the joys of the project. Before criticizing a pastor, missionary, or congregation, remember that while you are there, church life is going on. As one pastor said, "Tragedies are going on. I still have to minister to individuals in my congregation."

No Individuals Allowed

One missionary who handled teams in Africa said, "Americans are into individualism. When you join a team, you have to give up your rights as an individual. Privacy and individual rights are left at the airport. Volunteers must try to mold together as a team."

One boot camp for teens stresses, "There is no such thing as an individual; think as a team." Giving up the right to individualism in order to be part of a unified team is difficult for many North Americans. Equally difficult is the surrender of the right to be comfortable. Yet these are both part of the servant attitude required for serving on a mission team.

Model Cooperation

Effective ministry starts with a vital relationship to God and through caring relationships among team members. People everywhere are looking for something different. If they see team members arguing or fussing, they will have no attraction to Christ. It may take flexibility and a lot of grace, but always model cooperation, servanthood, and love in relationships with teammates and team leaders.

In speaking of servanthood, a mission team leader in Texas said, "The group is more important than the individual; the people you go to are more important than the group."

- Work together with the sponsoring pastor, missionary, or parachurch organization.
- There can only be one chief. No matter who you are, what you've done, or where you've been, be submissive to the team leader.
- Avoid judging the effectiveness of the ministry based on your short-term observations. It takes time to build trust in most areas.

- Avoid criticizing the use of funds. What may appear to be important to you may not be important there.
- Avoid criticizing a leader's tough or easy approach to a problem situation or individual. You may not know the whole story.
- Ask the host pastor or leader for direction in the use of literature in witnessing.
- Look for opportunities to help. Don't wait for orders.
- Avoid working with one group or insisting on doing only one job.

Comfort Cultures and Survival Cultures

In many cultures, people are content to survive. In our culture, survival is usually taken for granted. We use our energies to make the "best" better. We continually work to make the difficult easier and the uncomfortable more comfortable. If we are too hot, we turn on a fan or an air-conditioner. If the fan or air-conditioner isn't working we want to know why, and we call a technician. If we can't get the technician out immediately, we complain and call and threaten until we get service. In our culture, we do not suffer well.

Along with comfort, we want ease. The remote control for our home entertainment center is a monument to our love of ease and comfort. Our culture is dedicated to raising ease and comfort levels.

When you enter a survival-based culture, you won't readily shed your comfort-based culture. You will immediately begin, mentally, to make changes in your host culture. You will see difficulties that could be resolved and ways in which life could be made easier. When you cannot make the changes you visualize, you will be tempted to complain. Only when you approach the mission field with a proper understanding of your own cultural instincts can you then curtail those reactions which would create conflict on the field. In whatever uncomfortable situation you find yourself, you will have to make a conscious effort to accept the circumstances and stifle your complaints during the duration of your stay.

Only the Best

Of all the complaints, food is the subject of the most murmuring on the mission field. In our culture, we do not eat to survive. We eat for pleasure. We eat only the foods we like, and insist that all our food meets the world's highest standards for quality and purity. On the mission field, team members continue to approach their food from their North American cultural view. They look for pleasure in their food, not sustenance. When the food does not come up to their accustomed pleasure level, or does not stuff them to their limit, they complain. If you have difficulty with the food on the field, shift your cultural perspective. View food from a survival perspective rather than a pleasure perspective. The following scenarios were real situations.

Just Try It

As part of one tour, a mission director took the team to one of Jamaica's finer restaurants. Since the chef was noted for his Chinese cuisine, the director arranged for a variety of oriental dishes to be served family style. On the way to the restaurant there were a few murmurs about Chinese food, but the director assured the team that they would enjoy this restaurant and the food.

One volunteer emphatically said, "I do not like Chinese food."

"Even if you've tried Chinese and don't like it, you'll like this food," the director said.

"I have never eaten Chinese food, and I am not going to start now!" the man said.

In a setting of picturesque waterfalls, candlelight, and soft music, the team was served egg rolls, lo mein, chow mein, and some obviously oriental dishes. They were also served honey chicken, cashew chicken, shrimp, and beef dishes that were so Americanized, that they could hardly be called Chinese. Even those who had been hesitant to try Chinese took second helpings of the various dishes.

The one man, though, refused to allow a speck of food to be placed on his plate. As each dish passed by, he said, "I do not like Chinese food. I will not taste it. I want a peanut butter sandwich."

To be a useful part of a mission team, you must be flexible. When you are served food you don't like, take at least a little and try it. You don't have to heap the food on your plate. Eat just enough to be polite and graciously refuse seconds, without commenting on how you like or dislike the food.

Tips to Keep Chefs Happy

1. Try at least a bite of new foods. No one will force you to eat more. Try a bite, even if you have to quickly wash it down with drink.

2. Think before you speak. The cooks are doing their best. Cooking meals for 15 to 20 people, with a limited food budget, substandard food products, and semimodern conveniences is difficult. Keep the cook's feelings in mind when making comments about food.

3. Avoid statements like, "This would be perfect if we just had . . ." In small towns, be careful about complaints in restaurants. The waitress who you complain to will probably be related to a member of the church or the family to which you are trying to minister.

4. When serving yourself in a buffet line, don't think of the portions that those ahead of you took. Think of those behind you. If everyone takes the same size serving as you do, will there be food for the last person in line? After everyone is served, take a second helping if you like. Remember cooking facilities and transportation logistics may limit the food supply.

5. In a missionary guest house or home, you can be fairly well assured the food is safe. If you have questions about food in a local home or a restaurant, quietly and unobtrusively ask the missionary, "Is this OK?" If you feel a food is unsafe, or don't like it, quietly decline, or take a small serving and spread it around on your plate so that it appears you ate some.

6. Don't snoop in the kitchen, ask about the menu for the next meal, or give the cook suggestions for menus.

7. Never help yourself to food in the refrigerator or on the counter unless you have been told to do so.

8. Don't ask for snacks between meals. If you're hungry, eat the snacks you brought from home.

9. Eat the meal that is prepared. Unless you have made pre-arrangements about special dietary needs, don't ask for special meals. Some mission organizations ask about dietary restrictions when you register.

10. Avoid criticisms of a dish's nutritional value or fat content. A week of unhealthy eating won't kill you.

What's This?!

Some team members refuse to try different foods. Others will eat the food but complain about the menu or the way the food is cooked.

In a Guatemalan mountain village, water was finally restored to the work camp. The shower house was heaped with a week's laundry: mildewed towels, concrete crusted work clothes, and smelly socks and underwear. At dawn, I started washing clothes in order to get them dry before the late afternoon rains began. Instead of taking time out to prepare an American meal, I gave Noemi, my kitchen helper, instructions to cook a meal that she could handle easily: chili, rice, carrot salad, homemade bread, and a pudding. By late afternoon I was exhausted, but the washing was dry and folded. Happy with the day's work, I sat down to the meal Noemi had prepared.

One American looked at the food and said to me, "What's this?!" Turning to the other men at the table, he said, "You should see what my wife can do with food. She can take a little of nothing and transform it into a great tasting meal. You should taste her crab Newburg."

Be careful how you react to what is set before you. Even if the cook does not understand your words, he or she will often be able to read and interpret the subtle signals in your intonation and body language. Always express thanks and appreciation for any efforts made on your behalf.

But My Allergies!

Some team members use food allergies or dietary restrictions to manipulate the menus more to their liking.

"I have diabetes," one man said. "Those canned peas are loaded with sugar. Don't put those peas on my plate. You shouldn't serve us vegetables that have sugar added."

At the close of the meal, a chocolate cake was served. "Chocolate cake," the diabetic man exclaimed. "I've been hungry for chocolate. Give me that piece with the thick frosting."

Avoid attempts to hide your likes and dislikes with transparent excuses. Eat what is offered and always express your thanks.

It'll Kill Us All

On many teams, there is an all-knowing food sheriff who tries to manipulate menus with safe food rules. On one team, two men loudly proclaimed the dangers of lettuce. Although the lettuce had been disinfected, they publicly accused the missionary of serving dangerous food.

A few days later, a local resident brought a thank offering of strawberries to the camp. The missionary washed them and warned team members that they truly ate them at their own risk. (Unlike lettuce, strawberries could only be properly disinfected by cooking.) Guess who ate the most strawberries? You guessed it. The men who loudly claimed the lettuce would kill everyone.

Being careful about what you eat is sensible. However, try not to be offensive when you truly feel a food may be dangerous.

First in Line

Some volunteers never consider the needs of others on the team. On a long-term project, following the 1976 earthquake in Guatemala, I cooked for a continual flow of volunteers. Included in the relief supplies were tons of tuna and spinach. To make the spinach a little more palatable, I sliced boiled eggs across the top of the bowl of spinach. A couple of men passed the bowl. The third man scooped *all* the eggs off onto his plate.

On that project, the apartment-size stove limited the amount of food I could prepare for one meal. Without regard to the other 15 people behind them, 3 or 4 very hefty Americans—always first in line—would pile their plates with the main entree and ignore the side dishes. Those at the end of the line sometimes had to settle for bread and a couple of vegetables. The selfishness of team members such as these forced me to serve the food rather than allow self-service.

Some meals can only be treated with humor, but watch that the humor doesn't hurt someone. In one home, team members could hardly chew the tough goat meat. The team murmured jokes in English about the meat. When the hostess left the room, the missionary reminded them, "These people have spent a lot of money and gone to great pains to fix this meal. They understand more than you think. Treat the food respectfully and make your jokes later." You will find situations that call for hilarious one-liner comments. Store them in your memory. When the team is alone, you can entertain each other with your humorous observations.

In each scenario the volunteers involved acted selfishly. It makes no difference whether you are in a foreign country or in the US, whether you are eating in a restaurant or someone's home— wherever you are, remember to put the feelings and needs of others before your own feelings and needs.

Choosing the Better Seat

Another area in which team members have difficulties in modeling servanthood is in transportation.

Political upheaval in the Caribbean nation had created shortages of fuel. The missionary hired a driver to wait in the day-long-line to fill the truck tank and fill two five-gallon fuel cans. The precious fuel would be enough to travel to the next project, operate the generator for power tools, and return home.

When the project was completed and the missionary began loading the truck for the return trip home, one young man said, "I'm riding in the cab."

"There isn't enough room," the missionary said. "Edna and Eugene are older. They are exhausted and need to ride in the cab."

"Well, there's still room for one other person up front. I'm riding in front."

Patiently the missionary said, "You know that my wife has been sick. This is the first time she has been able to accompany a team for months. Riding in the back would be too hard on her. She needs to sit in the cab, too."

"I rode in the back on the way here," he said. "It's my turn to ride in the front!"

Angrily, the volunteer climbed into the back of the pickup truck. Shortly after the vehicle started down the road, the roof of the cab buckled and caved in. The missionary stopped the vehicle and ordered the young man off the roof of the cab. A few miles later, the missionary smelled gasoline. When he stopped to investigate, he found that one of the gasoline cans had turned over and the gasoline had leaked out in the truck bed.

"Didn't you notice that the gasoline was leaking out?" he asked the young man.

"I saw it," he said. "It fell over right after we left."

"Why didn't you set it up?"

He shrugged and said, "I was too tired."

On about the sixth day of a tour, the novelty of eating dust in the back of a pickup truck, or of bouncing on the back seat of the van, wears off and team members start jostling for the better seats. Be considerate of others in travel arrangements. Take your turn at sitting on the wheel wells of buses, in the back of pickups, and in the hard-to-get-to seats of the van. As a rule, transportation is going to be crowded. As one missionary said, "You must get used to the idea that your hips will touch and your knees will be even with your neck."

Reaching Goals

In our culture we value efficiency and production. Other cultures put more emphasis on relationships. Whether taking a mission awareness tour, conducting a Vacation Bible School, planting trees, giving vaccinations, or building a school, most team members have objectives in mind. They plan to visit eight mission projects, plant 5,000 seedlings, or raise the walls on a church. Having goals is commendable and gives team members a sense of direction. Completion of those goals, however, is not the most important objective of a mission tour. It is through good relationships that you will lead people to Christ. Establishing warm relationships and communicating the love of Christ is the team's primary goal. That goal should be kept in mind in all relationships: team members, pastoral staff, and local people.

Make your best preparations, then go with the flow. The prepared volunteer goes expecting the best, but accepting the possibilities of setbacks and disappointments.

When you arrive, nothing may be as you thought it would be. On construction projects, delays are caused by legal hassles, weather, material shortages, and labor problems. Delays and altered schedules require flexibility from volunteers. If possible, an advance visit to the site might eliminate many problems.

However, even with the best plans, setbacks will occur. Volunteers must be taught the true meaning of flexibility. One pastor said, "Volunteers believe they are flexible, but when they get to the project site, they realize they are not. The key to *flexibility*," he said, "is believing God is in control. We don't run the church like a business. Our projects are done more by prayer and following God, than by following a rigid schedule. It's God's program and schedule. Delays often bring a greater blessing down the road. It all works out in God's time."

If you are unable to do the work you came prepared to do, then do the job at hand. It is more important to do what needs to be done than to be only able or willing to do one thing. Avoid fretting and complaining. Accept the changes in your plans as coming from God, not coming from others. Be open to God's plan. Look for what God is trying to show you in the situation and how God is wanting to work through you.

One construction team, which included children, was switched to a retirement home. It seemed an impossible situation, but team members turned it into a blessing for all involved. When materials didn't arrive in time to reroof a church, team members worked on the home of an elderly member of the congregation. Team members who are open to new experiences often receive unusual blessings.

Chasing Gnats

If bugs, especially gnats, are bothering you, spray repellent on a cloth and stick it in your shirt pocket or under the edge of your hat band.

Tips for Work Teams

1. Pace yourself, especially if you have made drastic changes in climate or altitude or you have physical problems such as heart or lung trouble. You know what you can do, but don't be afraid to push a little beyond normal endurance. One team member said, "I found I could do more than I thought."

2. Accept the schedule. It may be a harried, nonstop schedule or one that seems never to get rolling. Relax, and do your best to go with the flow.

3. Do your assigned task the best you can.

4. Allow others to do their work in their own way. If you think your way is better, set an example, but don't tell others how to work.

5. Take orders from the designated leader. Avoid following team members who assume unassigned leadership roles.

6. Avoid comments such as, "We sure don't do it that way in . . ."

7. Accept unreached goals if necessary. Relationships are more important than goals.

8. No matter what your purpose or goal in going, take time to meet and communicate with people in the host country.

Facing Disappointments

One music evangelism team had spent eight days practicing, traveling, and conducting services. At night, mosquitoes and scurrying rats in the attic often kept them awake. At the close of their tour, they headed toward the mission headquarters and a well-deserved afternoon of relaxation on a nearby beach. Early in the morning the vehicle dropped a drive shaft on a curve in the mountains. The promised day of relaxation and fun in the sun was immediately canceled. In that remote area help would be hours away.

This team could have responded by grumbling, but they didn't. They sang to the people who had gathered around the disabled vehicle, and they fanned out across the nearby slopes to visit the scattered homes. In the afternoon, they bought fresh fruit from nearby stands and went to the local river *laundromat* to cool off. When that team finally boarded the bus to return to the city, the music leader said, "Today was the very best part of our tour. God truly blessed us by allowing us to meet these people. We had a wonderful day."

Advance preparation does not ensure a pleasant mission tour. Sometimes the tour is a fiasco. Inexperienced leaders may direct the team, materials for the project may not arrive, your luggage may get lost, the accommodations and food may be miserable. Other team members may have no spiritual or practical preparation. Furthermore, illnesses and accidents do happen. God doesn't always protect us from physical harm. If you find yourself on a disappointing tour, this is the time to make the proverbial *lemonade* from the lemons that life hands you.

Mission Field Lemonade
1. Resist the temptation to complain about not getting your money's worth. You came to serve, not receive.
2. Avoid jumping to conclusions about the reasons for the disastrous trip. You seldom know all the facts.
3. Avoid fretting and fuming.
4. Don't try to change fellow team members or circumstances. Simply concentrate on doing your job to the best of your ability.
5. Accept the situation as being allowed by God. Look for lessons and ways to make the situation better. Give God a chance to bring something good out of the situation.
6. Rely on God for strength, calmness, patience, and wisdom. Maintain a peaceful attitude toward all.
7. In the case of injury, follow the team leader or missionary's advice. Do not insist on staying if they feel you should return home.

Knowing how to respond positively to unpleasant situations takes some of the fear and frustration out of the situation. Often the teams that face the most setbacks, uncover the richest spiritual treasures. When the best logistical plans of a mission tour fall apart, look for God's better plan.

Get Acquainted with Everyone

Lifetime friendships are often formed on mission tours. To get the most out of a mission tour, avoid sitting with one person, one couple, or close friends all the time. On long bus rides, sit with someone you don't know well. Eat with a different person each day. Get to know every team member. Share stories of your spiritual journeys. You'll come home enriched by the fellowship with your teammates.

Look for ways to encourage team members who may be frightened, confused, or homesick. Some team members may struggle to meet unplanned expenses. If you know that a teammate is struggling financially, you may want to pick up a meal tab or offer to pay their way into a tourist attraction.

Before offering too much financial help, though, check first with the team leader. Sometimes the poverty of a team member may not be as it appears. On one tour, a woman told my husband and me that she would like to help a young man on the team who didn't have enough money to buy souvenirs. We laughed. We knew that the young man held a government position and probably had a higher salary than any of the other team members. He simply had no desire to buy cheap tourist trinkets.

In our culture, conversation is continually interrupted. In other cultures, people spend more time talking to each other. Without the diversions of phones, radios, and TVs, you will have time for long conversations with teammates.

Relationships

To accomplish the most and to get the most out of a volunteer mission experience, it is important to bond as a team. Bonding requires an effort to get to know people and some giving up of what we consider to be our rights.

Don't isolate yourself or pair off with friends. Work with different partners. Eat with different members of the team. Get to know everyone on the team.

Use common sense in male/female relationships. Be sure your conduct does not offend others and does not bring reproach on the organization you represent. As you get to know teammates better, you'll be more relaxed and casual in your conversation. To be a favorite conversational partner keep the Conversation Cues in mind.

Conversation Cues

- Avoid negative statements about religious organizations, doctrines, or politics.
- Avoid gossip.
- Avoid complaining.
- Avoid course jokes and sexual innuendo.
- Avoid probing other people's lives with the pretense of being a counselor.
- Avoid ethnic jokes.
- Avoid *telling all*.

A missionary in Africa said, "It seems that when people get far away from home and acquaintances they reveal the most sordid details of their churches and their lives." When you relate stories of abuse, addictions, illnesses, divorce, and other traumas, avoid the tabloid approach. Summarize problems. Save details to relate God's encouragement and deliverance in the situation. Sordid details will only depress people; spiritual lessons will encourage others.

When traveling, take time to talk with fellow team members. Tell about ways God has led you or encouraged you. Take time to review the day and make plans for the next day. Include humor in your conversation, but avoid humor that would hurt someone else. Try to encourage those who are homesick or discouraged. And most of all, listen; don't do all the talking.

Humor: When to Hold It, When to Let It Out

In college, I traveled on a spring tour with an a cappella choir. Each night, we stayed in a different home, where our evening meal was provided. We were expected to be gracious to the host family, no matter what accommodations or food was provided.

Each morning, though, when we boarded the bus, we eagerly

vied for the chance to tell our experiences. Even the bus driver and music director had stories. One quartet member had eagerly chosen a home with a beautiful girl. After the concert he was given only ice cream. Two other quartet members who had gone to a retired couple's home had been served a turkey dinner with all the trimmings. One person stayed in the home of a cuckoo-clock collector. (All the clocks worked, all night long.) Another had shared a room with an Airedale that kicked fleas and slurped water.

All of us kept our observations to ourselves while we were in the host home. Our first hour on the bus, though, was always a sharing time for the funny one-liners that we had held in while in the presence of the host family.

Humor will be a constant part of your mission field experience. At times, you may have a difficult time wiping a smirk off your face or choking down a chuckle. You will think of many funny responses to the new culture and the new situations in which you find yourself. The servant, though, places the feelings of those in the host culture ahead of his or her own desire to get a laugh. The servant waits until the appropriate time to express humor.

Avoid Attention-Getting Behavior

The maître d' assured the mission team that they would be seated as soon as tables were set in a private dining room. The main dining room reflected a restful ambience. Waiters and waitresses dressed in traditional costumes moved silently between candlelit tables. Organ music drifted across the room, muffling the clink of dinnerware but not intruding on intimate conversation.

Seeing the Americans, the organist drifted from a Spanish love song to a slow, popular, American tune.

"Amazing Grace!" one team member said. "He's playing 'Amazing Grace.' Let's go sing."

The team quickly surrounded the organist and began singing. The expressions of the diners ranged from amusement to consternation.

When the team members returned to the missionary, one team member exulted, "What a witness! God just gave us the chance to witness to all the people in this restaurant. Isn't God good?"

Americans have a tendency to draw attention to themselves. As one missionary said, "Volunteers have hearts of gold and work hard, but their boisterous conduct has often embarrassed me. They laugh loudly in restaurants and stagger through airports and streets acting as if they are drunk. I love them, but sometimes, they've made me want to crawl under the table."

Effective witnessing focuses attention on God, not the messenger. In the case of the team singing "Amazing Grace," only those in the restaurant who knew English or were familiar with the translated song understood the song. Others might have wondered if the team members had been drinking.

Witnessing can be done effectively in any setting if the volunteer is sensitive to the direction of the Holy Spirit. Some team witnessing, though, is a spur-of-the-moment reaction, rather than a Spirit-directed response. In most public areas, take your cue for conduct and witnessing from your surroundings. If the crowd is rowdy and loud, call out your favorite song, gather around the piano and sing. If the dining room is formal and the conversation and music subdued, make sure you have the Spirit's direction before launching into public witnessing. Whether you are in a foreign country or the United States, boisterous, attention-getting conduct does not exalt Christ.

Common Courtesies

1. Read the bulletin boards. Consult the schedule often. Don't rely on a teammate to keep you informed.
2. Be on time. Be on time for meals, devotions, and departures. You waste the entire team's time when they have to wait for you.
3. Attend all meetings. Participate in as many extra activities as you can.
4. Respect the needs of others for privacy, silence, and sleep. One girl got up at 3:00 A.M. to wash and blow-dry her hair. When her three sleeping roommates quietly complained, she said, "I know I won't have time in the morning, so I'm doing it now."
5. Bathe daily. One Canadian missionary said, "Some people from the north aren't used to bathing daily. They don't understand that they have to take a bath every day in the tropics." One man

wore one set of lightweight clothes every day. Each evening he hung his clothes out to dry. No, he didn't wash them. He just hung them out so that the perspiration could dry. To his teammates he bragged, "These are great clothes for the mission field. Quick drying. Never have to wash them."

6. Watch for annoying behavior in yourself. As the tour progresses, you'll find yourself mentally tagging team members. Common names for team members are The Lone Ranger (constantly leaving group to do what he wants to do), Motor Mouth (never quits talking), The Counselor (probes for dark secrets in order to offer advice and gossip), and the Joker (endless supply of jokes). These behaviors are tolerable at first, but they grow increasingly annoying as the days pass.

Mission Tour Veterans

If you have been on another mission tour, even in the same country and with the same organization, don't go expecting a replay of a past experience. If possible, renew old friendships, but don't nag a team leader to take you to meet old friends.

• Go with the intention of expanding your view and learning new things about your host country.

• Resist the urge to compare experiences, leaders, projects, and teams.

• Resist the temptation to be a self-appointed tour guide. One girl who had visited the field a couple of times kept up a steady travelogue about the country. When team members would ask the missionary questions, she would jump in with the answers— answers that were distorted sound bites of information. The missionary finally had to ask her to be silent because he couldn't converse with team members.

If you are a mission tour veteran, make sure each trip includes a stretching experience. Set new goals, learn more of the language, reach out to a different people group than you did on previous trips, or learn more about the history or culture of the host nation.

CHAPTER 19

In Search of a Real Missionary

When my husband and I were serving as full-time missionaries in Haiti, we took a group of volunteers to a remote area in northern Haiti. Another missionary, who had spent nearly 30 years in the country, accompanied us because he knew the area and the congregation.

During the team's stay, volunteers put up walls for a new church, gave their testimonies in church, and gathered each evening for a devotional and songfest with the local people. On one occasion, the team visited an American missionary couple who manned a transmitter for a Christian radio station. By the end of the tour, team members were excited about sharing missions in their home church.

On the way back to Port-au-Prince, where the team would depart, one middle-aged woman said, "This has been a wonderful experience. I guess that I just have one regret. I brought several packages of gelatin to give to a missionary family, but I never did get to meet a *real* missionary. I really had my heart set on meeting a *real* missionary."

After one team spent a week in a missionary home, a team member said with disdain to the wife, "You're no missionary. You're just a housewife and a mother."

Another visitor returned home to report the truth about what was happening in a mission organization. "Those people weren't spiritual," he said. "Some nights the missionary families got together and watched videos that had no religious content in them at all."

While on leave, one missionary's mother bought her several casual, attractive dresses. On the missionary's return to the field, she accompanied a mission team. Before she had a chance to unpack her clothes, she found a team member inspecting the contents of her suitcase. "Pretty good clothes for a missionary," the team member commented.

When the family of a newly married missionary visited her on the field, they brought a rocker and fancy needlepoint pillows to add a homey touch to her simple home. When she and her husband hosted a mission team, members murmured about the fancy furnishings and waste of money that could have fed orphans.

One missionary said, "For three years, we had no furniture. Our family of four kept all our belongings in boxes under the bed. Now that we have furniture and a place that my teenage son can invite friends to, I finally feel at home." She continued, "When we opened our home to share it with a mission team though, team members criticized us for our standard of living."

Mission Inspectors

Some team members feel responsible to evaluate the performance of mission organizations and missionaries and report their findings to anyone who will listen.

Assessments of mission work made by team members are often inaccurate because regular field activities must be curtailed in order to care for the team. Furthermore, team members who are trying to photograph the work of the missionaries forget that everything which is accomplished on the field cannot be photographed.

One missionary's wife was criticized by team members because she didn't travel with the team and help the women carry cement blocks and sift sand.

While the team was out, that missionary was handling all the local mission accounting, filing reports for mission headquarters, corresponding with several hundred churches and supporters, making out menus, and ordering food supplies for the next team.

Misconception: The Wedge Between Volunteers and Missionaries

Few missionaries will ever measure up to the *real* missionary image some volunteers bring to the mission field. In the past, missionaries could live up to the ideal image because their contact with supporters was limited to one or two hours during speaking engagements while on furlough. When supporters move in with the missionary for ten days, however, the true missionary is revealed. The realities of modern-day missions and missionaries often disillusion volunteers.

If mission teams are to be an effective link between the home church and the mission field, team members must go to the field with a realistic understanding of the modern missionary movement.

Changing Roles

The purpose of missions—world evangelism—has not changed, but the missionary's role in accomplishing that goal has changed. In the past, missionaries were Jacks- or Jills-of-all-trades. They could be found evangelizing, pastoring, teaching, pulling teeth, administering medicine, or overhauling an automobile.

In many places today, missionaries may serve in supportive roles and specialize in one field. The local Christians pastor, evangelize, and teach on the church level, while foreign missionaries serve as seminary teachers, mechanics, communication specialists, accountants, pilots, and builders.

There are still some *real* missionaries who hack their way through the jungle and brave poison arrows to deliver the gospel to *naked natives,* but those aren't the only real missionaries.

Changing Audience

Not only has the role of the missionary changed, the target audience has changed. The term *unreached* is not synonymous with uncivilized. Many of the unreached people groups of today live in towering condos and work in stock exchanges. Some operate lucrative businesses or hold government positions. To minister to the unreached groups, missionaries must live where the people live. Often that means living in a city of well over a million inhabitants.

The Suffering Missionary

Volunteers often arrive on the field with misconceptions about the missionary's lifestyle. There is no typical missionary lifestyle. Various influences shape the lifestyle of today's missionary.

Missionaries in primitive and rural areas will have fewer conveniences; their city counterparts who have electricity and supermarkets will have less peace and quiet. Each area has advantages and disadvantages. Location, however, is not dictated by a missionary's desires, but rather the needs on the field.

If team members arrive and see their missionary staggering in from a mass-baptismal service, his wife washing the garbage bags (for the 14th time), the children sweating with malaria chills, and the whole family eating rice and beans by lantern light, their hearts will well up with gratitude over the difference their sacrificial offering made.

If team members arrive on the field and see the missionaries they support cheering at their daughter's basketball game, eating pizza afterward, and going home to a house that overlooks the smog-bound city, they may be immensely disappointed. It's clear to these supporters that these aren't real missionaries because they aren't suffering.

Suffering Is Not Synonymous with Effectiveness

Missionaries do not take vows to suffer, but vows to serve. A certain amount of suffering is inescapable. At times the missionary may have to sleep on a bug-infested mat and eat guinea pig. These experiences, though, are usually rare and of short duration. If missionaries plan to stay in a primitive area for extended periods, they will most likely create a home by bringing in tents, generators, water purification systems, a communication system, and essentials for more comfortable accommodations.

The missionary who can come home at night to a mosquito-free environment, a shower, pure drinking water, familiar food, and a comfortable bed will have a longer, more productive career than the one who insists on sleeping on a mat in a thatched hut and eating out of a community kettle. The missionary who *never* has a retreat place often becomes a bitter missionary and quickly suffers burnout.

Family Matters

Just as parents in North America have encountered problems when sacrificing the family to make a business succeed, missionaries have faced the same problems. Earlier missionaries did great works, but some literally abandoned their families. The majority of missionaries' kids fared well, but some reacted bitterly to absentee fathers, nannies, and boarding schools.

Today, MKs (missionaries' kids) are often home schooled or attend English-speaking schools. Because of the benefits of an English-speaking education, mission schools draw students from the international community and the upper strata of society. In the large cities of the world, many of today's MKs attend school with the children of international diplomats and super-wealthy jet-setters. These MKs, like teens in North America, encounter peer pressure to indulge in alcohol, drugs, and promiscuous sex.

Most missionary mothers would love to do more mission work, but latchkey missionaries' kids, especially in cities, feel just as abandoned and are as susceptible to getting into trouble as latchkey kids in North America.

In recent years, the divorce rate has also increased among missionary couples. Today's missionary understands the importance of including family needs in the mission agenda.

On a Typical Day . . . You'll Wait in Line

In many ways, today's missionaries live much as team members do. They carpool kids to dental appointments, school functions, and youth outings. They wait in lines in traffic, at the bank, and at the supermarket. They contend with air pollution, traffic jams, crime, and no place for peace and quiet. They too struggle with issues such as staying within a budget, saving for their children's education, caring for elderly parents, and saving for retirement. At times the pace is nearly as frantic as in North America. During frequent electrical outages, water and food shortages, and political upheavals, their lives get even more hectic. To survive the pressures, missionaries need a means of rest and relaxation.

Not with My Money

In the past missionaries read the classics, practiced musical instruments, and played chess in their free time. Many volunteers expect to see modern missionaries relaxing in the same way. Today's missionary, however, will more likely be playing tennis, scuba diving, or playing a computer game.

Don't expect a missionary to spend every minute of every day evangelizing. The missionary that has a long productive ministry realizes the necessity of balance. Balance includes recreation, hobbies, and a relaxing home atmosphere. Their bookcases will hold many of the same books that your bookshelves hold.

A generation ago, many missionaries lived in a compound or on a campus which provided both a retreat from the pressures of cross-cultural ministry and room for their children to run and play. Outside the compound there were often opportunities to horseback ride, swim, play soccer, picnic, ride motorcycles, and hike. Today, those who live in rural areas still have these opportunities for recreation.

Many modern missionaries, however, rent apartments or small houses in cities where real estate is sold by the inch. Houses are built flush with the sidewalk or street. There is no room for softball or badminton games. Any extra space is used to park vehicles off the street. Furthermore, North American forms of public recreation such as bowling alleys, skating rinks, miniature and regular golf ranges, batting cages, go-carts, amusement parks, swimming pools, and playgrounds can only be found in resort areas.

To provide some means of recreation and relaxation, some

mission organizations in warmer climates provide a pool for city missionaries and for rural missionaries who visit the city periodically. In colder climates, the missionaries may belong to a health or athletic club. Preconceived images of missionaries seldom include visions of them sipping lemonade beside a pool or playing racquetball.

One team member, who lived on a scenic lake in Michigan, went in search of a missionary family which her church could support. Inquiring about one couple, she asked, "Does their apartment complex have a pool?" She continued by explaining, "I couldn't stand it if a missionary lived better than I did."

Where Did They Get the Money for That?!

Some volunteers have been upset about the extravagances of some missionaries. No matter how a missionary spends money, there will be supporters who believe it should have been used a different way.

First of all, no missionary who operates under a mission board is going to get rich on the mission field. Secondly, the missionary's salary leaves little room for many extravagances. As with all people, some missionaries handle money carelessly and get into debt. The end result, however, will not be an increase in pay but a ticket home to stay.

In many established mission organizations, missionaries live on a budget determined by the mission board. A certain amount is allocated for education, child care, housing, transportation, insurance, cost-of-living differential, food, and retirement. That budget provides for few extras. Some mission boards require that missionaries raise their own support package. Missionaries must take time from field work to raise support. Excess funds, raised during deputation are held in reserve for lean months. Any extra spending money will come from gifts from friends or relatives, holiday and birthday gifts, inheritances, or investments. Extra money does not come from other *mission funds*.

The way in which missionaries use expendable income is as varied as the personality of the individual. You'll find that missionaries spend money on clothes, furniture, books, education, long distance phone calls, eating out, vacations, electronic equipment and gadgets, trips back home, property, medical care, and investments. Actually, they spend money in much the same way as you do.

For what may appear to be an extravagance, there is a hidden trade-off. The person who eats rice and beans by lantern light may fly to the States for vacation each year. The person who buys a painting from an art gallery may seldom travel.

One boarding home for missionaries' kids had a pool. The upkeep on the pool put the missionary couple over budget, so they cut off the hot water heater. They traded hot showers for a pool. Often team members see only the extravagances; they do not see the trade-off to stay within budget.

Forging Links

The team member who goes to the field looking for a missionary that fits a certain mold will drive a wedge between the mission field and the home church. The team member who goes with a desire to learn about modern missions and missionaries will forge a solid link between the mission field and the home church. To forge strong bonds with missionaries:

- Trust and have faith in missionaries. If you are suspicious, they will sense it and will not feel comfortable sharing the problems and realities of the field with you.
- Avoid putting missionaries on a religious pedestal or telling them you admire them for their sacrificial life. Missionaries aren't looking for admiration or pity. They want respect as a professional and acceptance as an individual.
- Accept differences in temperaments, talents, gifts, and accomplishments among missionaries. Missionaries may be squeaky clean and organized or slovenly and pack rats. Some pour all their extra money back into ministry; others put it on a family vacation. Some may discipline their kids; others may let their kids run wild. Some are intense and hyper; others are laid-back, never hurried. Some are people oriented; others love books and computers. Some live simply; others need creature comforts. Some love sports; others would rather work crossword puzzles.

- Avoid judging the missionary's spirituality. When one missionary became agitated during a mildly turbulent flight in a small plane a volunteer muttered, "Some Christian. He sure doesn't have much faith." Years before, though, that missionary had been on a rough flight on a commercial passenger plane. Frightened, he had gotten off at the first stop. The plane had continued and crashed, killing all aboard.
- Take time to get acquainted with the missionary.
- Keep in mind that the missionary's regular workload may limit time with the team.
- Don't, however, constantly tell the missionary not to take time from the work to show you around. Let the missionary set the schedule.
- As you spend time with missionaries be sure to listen to their joys, burdens, concerns, and needs. Become part of their lives and ministry by affirming them. Remember they are separated from their families, and you can fill a real void in their lives by caring for them.
- Before you ask questions, take time to prepare yourself. Learn about the country, the specific work of the mission organization, and the individual missionary's work.
- Look for natural breaks in activities to ask questions.
- Don't ask questions that have no answers or have obvious answers. Questions such as "Why do they carry baskets on their heads?" have no answer. It's simply the way things are done. "Why do they dry clothes on bushes?" is obvious. They don't have dryers or clotheslines.
- Ask questions that arise naturally out of surrounding events. Ask questions about the upkeep of vehicles when you're on rugged mountain terrain, not when you're waiting for a church service to start.
- Don't be surprised if the missionary answers some questions with "I don't know."
- Don't be upset or surprised if the missionary does not comment on some of your observations and conclusions. Silence, a slight nod, or "Mmhuh" doesn't mean the missionary agrees; it is more often

a polite acknowledgment that you made a comment. Many team members have made observations, and because the missionary did not emphatically correct them, they have passed information on as quotes from the missionary. When you quote a missionary, be sure that the missionary spoke the words. Don't assume the missionary agrees with comments you or other team members make.

- Do not push your own ideas or agenda. Use your time to free the missionary and enable the missionary to push existing programs.
- Do ask the missionary to tell you about future projects and ask how you can help promote these projects.

Mind Your Manners

- Don't expect missionaries to be your maids. They aren't offering room service. One missionary said, "I love them, but they wear me out. I'm continually mopping spills, picking up soda cans and glasses, wiping wet spots off my furniture, and picking up towels."
- If your lodging is in a missionary (or national) home, remember **you are a houseguest.** This home has been opened to you. It is not a motel to be treated carelessly because you paid for the room.
- In whatever home you stay, treat the possessions of the owner with care. The home in which you stay may be furnished with locally crafted furniture. Some of this furniture isn't as sturdy as what you might find at home. Unlike casual furniture in our homes, it is varnished rather than protected by formica or polyurethane paint. Many missionaries have been heartsick to find wet towels draped over the backs of varnished dining room chairs, beverage glasses sitting in a puddle of water on mahogany end tables and bookcases, and suitcase scrapes on dresser tops. In one guest house, two very heavy girls sat on a couch and collapsed it. Instead of choosing seating that would hold their weight, they sat together on another couch and broke it too. The furniture may not look like much to you but it is their very best. Ask for coasters; put a towel under your luggage; test a fragile chair before plopping down in it. Always leave a home and the furnishings in as good a condition as you found them.
- Recognize the personal needs of the missionary, such as need for family time. If the setting is in a remote area, or the missionaries

seldom see friends from home, they will spend almost every waking hour with team members. If the missionaries handle mission teams constantly, they will need time alone and time with their family.

- In seating arrangements, don't grab the seat beside the missionary until you know where the spouse is sitting.
- Don't monopolize the missionaries. Allow other team members to sit with them and ask questions.
- Don't criticize or gossip about other missionaries.
- Don't try to catch the missionaries up on all the latest moral failures and church divisions at home.
- Be sensitive to single missionaries. Teasing and joking about their need to find a mate is always out of order.
- Don't complain if the missionary's bed or air mattress is better than yours. Remember, this is the missionary's day-in and day-out accommodations. You'll be home and in your comfortable waterbed next week.
- Don't plan for side trips to see friends, sponsored children, or other mission works, unless you've made arrangements ahead of time. On any extra trip, always pay for transportation costs and meals for the driver or interpreter.
- Don't feel you have to apologize for spending money. Missionaries aren't envious or displeased with your purchases if they do not dishonor the Lord.
- If a missionary accompanies you on an outing or excursion, team members should pay for the missionary's entry fees and meals. The missionary is only going as a guide and has probably been there several times already. This does not apply to scheduled outings on all-inclusive tours.
- If you feel you need to know a missionary's salary, check with mission headquarters at the home base. It is simply bad manners to ask someone about their salary or the cost of personal purchases they've made.
- Avoid remarks about wishing you were rich and could afford *servants*. Many missionaries would rather do their own household and yard work, but they hire employees in order to have time for mission work.

- Always be in subjection to the missionary. Obey, then ask questions later. This is especially important in areas of political instability.
- Accept the supervision of the missionary, even if you feel you are more qualified to direct a project.
- Avoid the phrase, "This isn't the way we do it in . . ."
- Take time to admire the missionary's collected curios and ask about their significance.[1]

Nothing to Do

One summer my husband and I visited a Bahamian mission station. Walking up from the road, we passed a washhouse piled with dirty clothes and crossed a patch of knee-high weeds to get to the mission house. A mission volunteer sat on the veranda reading a book. When we asked what she was doing that summer, she replied, "Not much. I've been very disappointed. I came here expecting to do missionary work, but they don't seem to have anything for me to do." Inside the house, she escorted us across a gritty tile floor to our room, then returned to her rocker on the veranda.

If you don't have a clear assignment, look for ways to help. I will always remember the young man who saw me trying to figure out how to cut chickens. He simply walked into the kitchen, took the knife and said, "I can do that. I used to be a meat cutter." In five minutes, he had cut all the chickens. I would have never thought to ask a team member to do that job, but he saw a job that he could do and he did it. Look for needs that no one is filling, but which you can meet. Ask if you can help. If your offer is refused, don't push. Most likely, though, your offer will be accepted and long remembered.

Some of the ways in which team members can give missionaries a hand include mailing letters and packages in the US, cutting or perming hair, mending clothes, addressing envelopes, making sandwiches, repairing small appliances, making minor house repairs, gardening, taking missionaries' kids on outings, or baby-sitting in order to give the missionary couple a night out.

In helping, take into consideration what needs to be done, what you can do well, and what the missionary wants done. Do not tear down machinery or vehicles unless you have replacement parts on hand for the repairs. Never assume that you can find a needed tool or part.

Also, keep your eye open to opportunities to help the missionary after you return home. What are their hobbies and tastes in music and books? Would they enjoy a subscription to a magazine on writing, woodworking, or gourmet cooking? What interests do their children have?

Promises. Promises.

Missionaries who handle teams on a regular basis have learned that volunteers who promise to send items from home to the mission field seldom keep their promises. To avoid misunderstandings, do not make promises to missionaries.

Team members do not intend to break their promises, but once they return to their own culture the needs of the foreign culture and missionaries fade. Instead of making promises, ask if the missionary could use an item, and ask how the item could best be sent. Preface your question with "I can't make any promises, but I may be able to send you . . ."

It is important that you check with the missionary before sending any item. The custom's duty may be higher than the value of the item. When one team heard that my husband liked root beer, they sent us six cans. The custom's duty was $2 per can. Before sending anything, make sure it is wanted and ask about the best way to send it.

If you do plan to send something to the missionary, write yourself a *big* note so that you won't forget.

When the Sad Facts
Are Too Obvious to Be Denied

If you feel you should evaluate the return on your missionary dollars, do not look at the missionary. Look at the end result, the local church. Don't pick at every little thing the missionary purchases with your money; instead, look at whether or not it enables the missionary to birth and nurture the national church. If that church is a vital, growing force in the community, then your dollars were well invested.

On the other hand, your money may be supporting an incredibly frugal missionary, who has never thrown away a glass jar, but whose ministry has not resulted in any new lives for Christ in the last 20 years. If this is the case, your mission dollars have probably been wasted. Look at the health of the national church to determine the success of missions.

Occasionally, team members find good reason to be disillusioned on the field. A music team toured Haiti one summer. Several members from Texas asked to visit an independent church and a national pastor whom they had adopted as their missionary and had supported for years. Since their support had been substantial, they wanted to see firsthand where their mission dollars had gone.

When the missionary tried to set an appointment with the pastor, he was always out. Finally, after several attempts, the missionary located the pastor's residence. He lived in a house and drove a vehicle that seemed beyond the means of most local pastors, even those who received help from the States. The pastor did not seem eager to meet the team, but gave directions to the church.

On Sunday morning, the Texas team members could hardly wait to meet their pastor and his people. When they arrived, they found a one-room, unpainted building surrounded by weeds. Twenty or so people were scattered across the unswept room. The people did not sit in clumps as families in congregations do. They appeared to be unrelated, unacquainted people who had been called in from the street to sit on the peeling benches. There was no interaction between pastor and people; no one seemed to know him. The audience had no idea how to participate in worship. It was clearly a staged service. On the trip home from the church, the Texas people asked, "Where did all the money go? We've been sending money here for years."

A hundred miles from that location, four Haitian brothers who are pastors live in modern homes and drive fairly new vehicles. They too are missionaries who receive financial support from the States. Together, though, they have established over a hundred churches which are filled to capacity and explode with vibrant, enthusiastic worship every Sunday morning. These brothers open their churches, schools, and feeding programs to the constant scrutiny of mission teams. When you evaluate the investment of mission dollars, look at the end result—look at the spiritual health of the national church.

If the health of the national church does not appear to be good, and you feel concerned about the use of mission dollars, use these guidelines to further evaluate the work.

- Are the leaders willing to communicate with team members concerning their goals, successes, and failures?
- Are the leaders working with a resistant target group? Some people groups do not respond quickly to the gospel. Lack of response does not mean lack of effort on the part of the missionary.
- How does the missionary interact with family members, local church leaders, other missionaries within the organization, and business associates? These are the people that see how the missionary lives when you are gone. If the missionary has a self-serving attitude and ignores the needs of others, their responses will reveal this. If the people around the missionary are respectful and supportive, then your concerns are probably unfounded.
- How does the missionary relate to missionaries in other organizations? Be cautious about supporting any missionary who tears down the work of another missionary or claims to be more sacrificial or spiritual than other missionaries.
- Do the missionaries share what they have with others? Older missionaries constantly counsel new missionaries, "Don't apologize for what you have. Just be willing to share what you have with others." This doesn't mean that the missionaries invite people off the street for dinner each night or that they pass out their CDs on the street. It does mean that they open their home to neighbors, missionaries' kids, local church members, and national pastors.

Real Missionaries

Team members who can set aside preconceived ideas about missions and missionaries can play an important role in global missions. They can effectively link the mission field to the home church by bringing home a *real* image of missionaries and missions.

CHAPTER 20

Love in Any Language

Developing positive relationships with the national or local church starts with good relationships among team members, team leaders, and missionaries. Bad attitudes and tense relationships translate to any language. Love and unselfishness also translate.

One requirement for building solid cross-cultural relationships is a servant attitude. This isn't a subservient attitude, but rather a setting aside of our North American attitudes of superiority and defense of individual rights. In addition, the servant-minded team member will need to focus on the importance of people.

The team member who accepts and values each person, despite moral problems and differing opinions, will find open doors in any culture. Team members who show honor and respect to people of other cultures will usually find their cultural blunders are overlooked.

Appearances Are Deceiving

As you study the local people and the culture, keep in mind that a nation's culture is far more complex than it appears. Africa has both warring tribes and sophisticated professionals. At first glance, Filipinos, many of whom speak English, appear to embrace American culture; a closer look into intricate relationships reveals an Oriental mind-set. Even in the United States, local cultures are extremely complex. Never make assumptions about a culture, whether here in the US or abroad.

In many nations, especially in Asian countries, conflict situations are handled so that no one loses face. This is difficult for North Americans who *must* determine who is at fault and publicize the findings.

Observe rather than offer solutions. No problem is as simple as it appears. When a team visited a village in Africa, they found nearly everyone ill. The team members went home and raised funds to build and staff a hospital. When members returned a couple of years later, the villagers' health had not changed. The problem was bad water. They needed a new well, not a hospital.

Personal Evangelism

When materials are provided or services are rendered, it is important that the volunteer does not obligate non-Christian recipients to accept the gospel. To avoid this:

- Show a genuine interest in the person whether they care about God or the church.
- Avoid preaching to them or telling them how they should live.
- Look for a common point of interest: sports, quilting, canning, fishing, etc.
- Be ready to give an answer concerning the spiritual life you have. Sooner or later, you will be asked, "Why? Why are you here? Why are you different?"
- Avoid pointing to yourself as a hero. Point to Christ as your helper. Emphasize your desire to share what Christ has given you.
- If the person mentions a personal or family problem, offer to stop and pray with the person about the need.

- Before you leave, assure those to whom you witnessed that you will keep them in your prayers.
- Keep in touch with the people after you go home.

"I'm an American."

Avoid the phrase, "I'm an American." People who live in Central and South America are Americans also. Say instead, "I'm from the States" or "the US" or "North America."

Be careful how you refer to the local people, especially in public meetings or discussions with the local people. Do not refer to tribal or ethnic names until you know it is appropriate. In Rwanda, a visitor was rebuked for referring to the people by their tribal names. The visitor was instead told to refer to them as *shorts* or *talls*. The missionary can advise you on this. If in doubt, calling the local people by their national name such as *Jamaicans* or *Bolivians* is always appropriate. Never call them *natives* or *heathen*.

We're Number One

Avoid comparison conversations that exalt your country, state, or culture over another. Encourage the youth to take advantage of all the opportunities in their own area, rather than tell them how much better they could live where you come from. Guard against a superior attitude in regard to your education, possessions, and spiritual life.

Avoid acting toward others as if they are ignorant or inferior. Avoid a condescending attitude by either overdressing or underdressing.

Look for similarities in your culture and the one you visit. Similarities, not differences, forge cross-cultural bonds.

Equalizers

If a custom seems unfair, unequal, or unjust don't jump in and try to equalize the situation. In Haiti, we had an excellent staff of cook, yard worker, housekeeper, and laundress. Some team members were upset when the staff did not sit at the long dining table and eat with the team. Some volunteers interpreted the seating arrangement as signs of class distinction and racial prejudice. We viewed the seating arrangement from a different perspective.

When lunchtime came, our staff served the food, then heaped their plates and went outside to eat. Their laughter and the sounds of a transistor radio always wafted through the windows. I knew our employees were getting a much deserved, relaxing lunch break. The staff would have been very uncomfortable sitting at a table with strangers and trying to handle their utensils correctly.

In a different setting, however, they would be comfortable sharing a meal with team members. When one team traveled to a primitive island, the cook accompanied us. At mealtime, everyone filled their plates and ate sitting on scattered stumps or crude benches. In that setting, where team members ate in smaller groups, and where table manners weren't so formal, the cook felt comfortable eating with team members.

Be careful how you refer to members of the missionary house staff. Never call them servants. Avoid the word *maid*, also. Refer to them by name or by position: cook, housekeeper, laundress, or yardman.

Learn the meaning of the word *yes* in each country. A nodding head or a *yes* may mean, *I hear you* or *I agree with you.*

Do not get involved or take sides in arguments, fights, or disputes among the local people. One night a volunteer found a woman crying alongside the road. He jumped to the conclusion that a guide who accompanied our team had abused the woman. He began questioning the woman in English. She, not understanding a word, nodded and kept weeping.

The team member beat on our door, awakening us and demanding that we kick the guide out of camp and have him arrested. When my husband located the woman, he spoke to her in Creole. She said that after an argument, her husband had made her get out of the truck. She was sitting alongside the road, waiting for a bus.

Avoid making judgments about racial prejudice. In many countries color is not an issue. Prejudicial divisions in other countries fall more along ethnic or social lines. No matter how you feel, do not voice your opinions about interracial or cross-cultural marriages; keep your opinion to yourself while on the field.

Avoid judgmental comments. Men in many countries hold hands as a gesture of friendship.

Respect Taboos and Customs

Avoid the taboos as much as possible. In Haiti, men do not cross their legs because they don't want the soles of their shoes to show. In India, people do not touch hands or hug. The missionary will inform you about the most common taboos.

Respect religious customs. You may witness a parade venerating a deity or saint. Be careful about comments, photography, and actions that would disrupt the procession.

In many nations, male and female relationships are not as casual as they are in North America. Women should be careful about initiating conversations with men. Always follow the missionary or team leaders' instructions about male/female relationships.

In both the US and abroad, avoid discussions of local politics, and the use of profanity, illegal drugs, and alcohol. As obvious as these admonitions are, some mission teams still have to deal with such issues among team members. The use of tobacco is also prohibited by social customs in many areas.

Be considerate when taking photos. Pass up a photo opportunity rather than offend. Focus more on positive aspects of the culture rather than misery and suffering.

Always be sensitive to local social mores. They will vary from city to rural areas, from east to west, from north to south, and from country to country.

Social Calls

Don't expect all homes to be primitive. Homes in Africa, South America, and many other places may be quite modern. Many residents live on a similar level of society to that in the US. When some team members have realized how wealthy and how advanced some countries were they have said, "Let them get their own missionaries." The Great Commission was not a command to go to those who were poorer or less educated than we, but to those who had not received the gospel.

If you are invited to the home of a local person for a meal or an evening of fellowship, a small gift is often appropriate; in some countries it is expected. In tropical climates, avoid chocolates. A small homemade craft would be appropriate in any culture.

Do take time to greet people properly. This may include an embrace, a kiss, or a handshake. Ask about the proper way to greet others. Don't rush in with an embrace if others bow to each other.

When you leave a home, take time to say good-bye. If you have met other members of the family, speak to them also.

In a social situation, you may be given drink or food that you know is unsafe. Watch the missionary for guidance. Often, a gesture toward eating or partaking is enough. One couple was presented water in every home that they visited in India. They graciously accepted each gift. After conversing a while, they put the water to their lips, then quietly placed the glass on the floor signifying they had finished.

Always be very careful about responses to food. Do not make casual jokes about the food in the presence of your hosts. Jokes, laughs, mumbled comments, and rolling eyes do translate into attitudes that can be read in any language.

Keep just a touch of formality in your relationships with the local people. In our culture we share our deepest darkest secrets on national TV and make public jokes about stupid things we've done. People in other cultures are more concerned about saving face or preserving dignity.

On one occasion, a brush arbor collapsed on one of our teams while we were eating. I found it hilarious, until my husband quietly said, "Don't laugh, these people are terribly embarrassed by this." To me, it was just another mishap, but to our hosts it was the collapse of their best preparations.

Show interest in the people's daily life. Let them show you how to weave or make pottery. Ask how a favorite food is cooked. Play their homemade musical instruments.

Working Together

On working projects (construction, outreach, medical, etc.), keep in mind "It's better to work together in harmony than to complete the job." Working with people, their way and at their pace, is more important than showing them new ways.

Go Tell It

- Have a written outline or copy of testimony in hand.
- Go over the outline with the interpreter before the service. Be sure to include any illustrations.
- Give the interpreter any Scripture reference you plan to use.
- Open with a greeting in the language of the people.
- Thank the people or compliment them about something in particular. (Kindness, attractive church, landscaping, an attraction in the city, etc.)
- Use your notes in order to keep your train of thought.
- Avoid the most common mistake—**do not listen to the translator,** but rather focus on what you intend to say next.
- Don't hurry.
- Face the crowd, not the translator.
- Unless the interpreter directs you otherwise, use short phrases or sentences. Avoid lots of conjunctions.
- Let the translator read Scripture passages in the local language.
- At the close, thank the audience for allowing you to speak.
- Thank the interpreter.[1]

Never give handouts. Give tips for small services rendered. Let someone carry a package, act as tour guide, shine shoes, or run an errand.

If You Encounter a Negative Reception

Though these pointers are directed to those working on construction teams, many of these suggestions apply to any mission trip. Keep in mind:

- A great deal goes on behind the scenes in a church regarding relationships and church programs.
- Any new ideas for outreach or expansion will have its critics. Some members may not be happy about the construction or evangelism project.
- The churches with which you will work do not have million-dollar budgets. These will likely be grassroots projects that stretch

everyone physically, financially, and spiritually. No matter the size of the church budget, building programs are stressful to everyone involved.

- Some construction or renovation projects are necessary because of rapid growth. This means many in the church are new converts and unfamiliar with donating time and money to the kingdom of God.
- Among those who attend the church, there may be an attitude of protectionism. Craftsmen in the congregation who take pride in the appearance of their church may oppose the shoddy work of some volunteers who are more interested in production than quality.
- The pastor may be distressed because the congregation doesn't help. The congregation may be embarrassed because the pastor never lifts a paintbrush.
- If there appears to be internal conflict, don't take sides on issues. **Do not be a part of the problem.**
- Don't discuss any negative observations with others. Churches tend to have family cliques.
- Every place is unique. If you have a bad trip, don't go expecting it to happen again.

As one team leader said, "A building program is a time when Satan can drive in wedges and destroy the work. He can rob the situation of joy." This is the time for volunteers to be sensitive to the Spirit's leading in overcoming setbacks and disappointments.

There are many ways in which volunteers can encourage a church during the high-pressure days of expansion or construction programs.

Encouraging the Congregation
- Use your talents. Don't be pushy, but let the pastor know if you can help with children's ministries, music, or youth work. If you have an interesting personal testimony, offer to share it in small group settings.
- If the church has a day care or Christian school, offer to share your talents during craft time or in a chapel service.
- Attend regular services on Sunday and midweek.

- Reach out to people, even if they don't respond.
- Try to work with people in the church. It is important to relate as workers *together*, rather than givers and receivers.
- Encourage the congregation. If the project is behind schedule, some may be discouraged and wish the project had never been started.
- Don't expect others to change their plans to spend time with you. You won't find much flexibility in church and family schedules. It will be your responsibility to establish relationships during your short stay.
- Join a local family in an activity, such as an athletic event, school pageant, or civic event.
- Take time to join a church activity. Women, take an afternoon off from sanding and painting to attend an aerobics class or Bible study. Men, attend the Men's Prayer Breakfast on Saturday morning. Quit early and play basketball with the youth group.
- If the church has an athletic team, go to the game and cheer loudly. It's more important to build relationships with the congregation than to get that last coat of paint on the baseboards.
- Take an afternoon to visit shut-in church members or those in retirement or nursing homes. Take along a small craft, bookmark, or plant to cheer those who are ill.

Construction Teams
in the United States: "Me Do It!"

Some of these teams are highly organized. Others may be loosely organized—put together on the spot with whoever shows up. Some teams come from a single church or locale; other teams are made up of volunteers from many states who arrive at the project site on a set date.

Problems with accommodations, food, personal safety, safety of possessions, and health hazards are minimal in these settings. However, of all the mission opportunities, team members are probably the *least prepared* to minister on these teams.

Have you ever tried to help toddlers with jobs that were just a little beyond their abilities? They yank the object from your hand

and say, "Me do it." Volunteers who work in the US with people above the poverty level tend to approach the tour with *me do it* attitudes. They have complete confidence that they can speak the language, do the work, and relate to the people. They don't need and don't want instructions.

Unless volunteers have advance preparation, however, they can be greatly disillusioned by the home mission experience. Personnel conflicts tend to be a little sharper here than on the foreign field because volunteers feel competent to handle any situation. Also, volunteers have certain expectations for brothers and sisters in Christ, especially those from one's own denomination. They measure both fellow teammates and the host congregation against that rule of expectation.

To the unprepared volunteer, the first surprise may come in choosing a date to help. Your offer to come on a certain weekend to roof the church addition or conduct a neighborhood survey may be turned down because the church has a picnic planned or the pastor will be out of town. Some volunteers have been upset when a church would not work with their schedule. In most cases, the volunteer works with the church's schedule; the church does not change its schedule for the volunteers. During a construction period, which could range from 40 to 120 weeks, scores of subcontractors, tradesmen, and volunteers flow through a construction project. Paid contractors and laborers receive priority in scheduling. Volunteers are plugged into the construction program wherever, whenever, and however possible.

Even though the project leader may have given you a date and a job description, be sure to check with the leader two or three days before going. The project may have been delayed or gotten ahead (not likely) of schedule. If so, the needs may have changed. With updated knowledge, you'll be able to take exactly the tools and material you will need. Many volunteers have arrived to find plans changed. Often they have said, "If I had known we were going to be doing this, I would have brought . . ."

Construction Manners

- Allow others to do their work in their own way. If you think

> ### *Congregation to Congregation Giving*
> Bibles
> Hymnals
> Literature
> Scholarships
> Church furnishings
> Communion sets
> Floral arrangements
> Gas lanterns
> Musical instruments—guitars, accordions, trumpets
> PA systems (battery-powered)
> Portable stereo (tape deck for background accompaniment)
> Typewriters, computers
> Athletic equipment (soccer balls almost always appropriate)
> Tracts
> Educational toys for nursery or day school (Before putting together school boxes, check with the missionary. Paper ruling varies from country to country.)
> Money (Sometimes the home church will send funds with the team to be used for special needs such as building materials.)

your way is better, set an example, but don't tell others how to work unless you are the designated leader.

- Take orders from the designated leader. Avoid following team members who assume unassigned leadership roles.
- If you are a skilled craftsman, be considerate about giving unskilled help a chance to work. Have them work with you, and instruct them in a kind manner.
- Know the construction philosophy of the church. Do they want production or quality? Leaders from one congregation clashed with volunteers who were doing electrical wiring. To save time and complete the project before they left, the volunteers wanted to run wiring diagonally through the attic area. The local people insisted that the wiring be squared and follow wall lines.

- Keep in mind, you can do more than you think you can do. One pastor who had done a lot of physical labor on a construction project said, "People can do more than what they think they can. I never dreamed I could help pour concrete, but when the time came and we needed help, I did it."
- If you know that you cannot do a job well, let someone else do it. Although you may be willing to try to do something new, there are some things each one of us has learned that we cannot do well. This is especially true of painting. If you can't paint well, offer to sand, scrape, set nails, or clean up after painters.
- Avoid comments like, "We sure don't do it that way in . . ."
- Accept unreached goals. Building relationships is more important than building sanctuaries.
- Take time to enjoy fellowship with the people around you.

Always Pay Your Own Way

If a national pastor or local layperson has helped with transportation, meals, phone calls, or any other team expenses, **make sure that person is fully reimbursed.** What may seem a small expense to you may be a day's wage to him.

Ministry Among the Poor

Unless advised differently, members of teams to impoverished areas should plan to be self-sufficient. This especially means taking in necessary food. If team members will be preparing meals, ask the team leader about bringing grills, camp stoves, cookware, and utensils. The local people may provide a special welcoming or farewell meal, but don't expect them to supply your daily fare. It's simply too big of a financial burden for the local people.

Accommodations are usually in recreational vehicles, campers, or church facilities. You will need to supply your own bedding and linens. Take toilet tissue and paper towels along, also. If you are in a foreign country, take enough money to purchase such supplies before leaving the last major city on your itinerary.

Don't promise to call home. You may not be near a phone. If it's summer and you'll be working outside, take insect repellent, hats, and sunscreen.

Crime, especially personal injury crime, is rare, but take proper care of your possessions. Put purses, cameras, and electronic gadgets out of sight unless you're using them.

If you leave the project area, go with a friend and let a leader know when you expect to return. In some remote areas, you could easily get lost.

Survival, Superstitions, and Suspicions

On home mission projects you will enter new cultures. It is more important to be a student than a teacher. Go with an open mind. For the most part you will be entering survival-based cultures. Most volunteers live in comfort-based cultures. In comfort-based cultures, people feel they deserve better, and they spend lifetimes trying to obtain a *better* house, car, boat, etc. Those who live in survival cultures spend their lifetime trying to provide food and shelter for their families.

In remote areas, you'll come in contact with superstition in daily life. If a local person stops you from an action that seems insignificant, take heed. In some mountain areas, simply taking a hoe into a house would signify impending death. Respect the superstitions and beliefs of others, even if you consider them unfounded and foolish.

In many areas you'll meet a mixture of suspicion and warm hospitality. Strangers, especially *uppity* people who use big words, drive big cars, and wear lots of jewelry and makeup are suspect.

Advance Cultural Studies

Because of limited entertainment and lack of writing skills, storytelling thrives in impoverished areas. A good storyteller will have a team laughing uproariously and crying too. With permission, tape some of the folklore and local music.

Ask about the early settling of the area. Don't push for information, but ask questions that naturally develop out of a situation. Ask about the history of the home or church on which you are working.

When was it built? By whom? What did the owners do for a living? One woman told how her father had made a living in the mountains of Kentucky by backpacking treadle sewing machines up to remote cabins. Be sure to learn everything you can from your host culture.

Home Improvement

Along with learning, you'll need to do the project you came to do. If you are on a construction project, you'll find incredible building code violations. Be careful when talking about construction methods and materials. Your first reaction will probably be to bulldoze the existing structure and rebuild. This usually isn't an option among the poor. They must have a home now, and they can't make payments, even minimal payments, on construction loans.

The dilapidated conditions of the homes are most often due to lack of funds and know-how than lack of ambition. The people simply do not have the money to buy proper building and patching materials for their homes. Hiring a qualified builder is totally out of the question.

In replacing a roof, one volunteer found that the home owner had insulated the roof with thick scraps of quilted jacket material which he had scavenged from a sewing factory. When the volunteer expressed surprise, an older man who lived nearby quietly said, "He did the best he could with what he had."

If you are doing home repairs, try to do the job that the owner wants done. Sometimes, however, the condition of the house may make this impossible.

One person wanted windows opened, which she had painted shut. Close examination of the windows revealed a rotted window casing. Closer examination revealed that the area around the casings had deteriorated. Opening the window would have created a dominoing need for repairs which were beyond the worker's ability, budget, and time limit. Before tackling any project on a run-down structure, evaluate how the repair will effect other structural deficiencies.

Get permission before discarding anything. You may want to attack a place with a shovel, but you may be throwing away memories that someone treasures.

Vacation Bible School Teams

Plan activities for adults who attend. In thinly populated areas where adults bring children from a distance, they must wait to take the children home. Make the waiting time a productive, enjoyable time by conducting a short Bible study and a craft session for the adults.

But They Are So Needy . . .

Limit personal giving to individuals, and give small mementos such as photos, postcards, key chains, bookmarks. All other giving should be anonymous and go through the local church, missionary, or organization.

If you are given a gift that you know is being given at great sacrifice, graciously accept the gift. You may feel better by refusing the gift, but set aside your own need to feel good. The giver's feelings are more important. (Read the following sections: Warm Fuzzies, Giving to Children, Appropriate Personal Giving, and It Is Better to Receive.)

Spiritual Life on the Field

Time for private devotions will often be hard to find. Take your moments as they come. Don't expect to have time each morning; your moments may come in the afternoon or evening. If you have taken time in the months preceding the tour to prepare spiritually, you will be well prepared.

See God as bigger than any situation. Look for His solution to problems. Expect to see God at work around you.

Avoid judging a person or an action as demon inspired. Demon possession is real, but leave that aspect of missions in the hands of missionaries.

Lay aside Christian liberties for the sake of local Christians. In India, one woman noticed that each time she placed her Bible on the ground, the local pastor picked it up. To him, the Word of God was too sacred to place on the ground. Be sensitive to what offends those around you.

Be careful how you spend, talk, and act around the local people. They assume that each team member is a mature Christian. Whether you like it or not, they tend to put you on a pedestal because you are bearers of the Word of God.

Don't give excessive praise to any one local person or take sides with a disgruntled church member. The person who may appear to be overlooked or treated unjustly may be one who has committed a grave sin and is on probation.

Church Services

In church, you will be given front choice seats. Others may be bumped from their front row seats to accommodate you. Although this practice may upset you, graciously accept the seat arrangement. Be pleasant at all times, especially when you are seated on a platform. Your reactions and countenance can be a positive or negative witness. Avoid whispering, raising eyebrows, or rolling your eyes at unusual situations. Although the setting may appear to be noisy and even a little chaotic, try to keep a reverent attitude.

Following a church service, avoid standing in groups with team members. Move through the congregation, greeting as many people as possible. Be sure to greet all age groups. If someone gave up a choice seat for you, be sure to thank the person.

Preachers

On one occasion, a minister who held a doctoral degree and pastored a large south Florida church preached in a rural church in Haiti. He wrote out his sermon and talked to the interpreter ahead of time about the message. The Haitian interpreter, inspired by the message, preached the message as if it were his own. In turn, the translator's enthusiasm fired the visiting minister. During the delivery, the minister and the translator moved so in sync that they almost seemed to breathe together. Team members were awestruck. They whispered, "We've never heard John preach like this before."

Notes and advance preparation will not restrict the work of the Holy Spirit. Lack of preparation and confusion in translation will limit the effectiveness of your message.

Ministers should not insist on preaching on the mission field.

Two pastors came on one team and both demanded a chance to preach. Since the tour was not an evangelistic tour, the missionary had to make special arrangements to accommodate the ministers. If you are a minister and would like to preach on the field, let the missionary know ahead of time that you are available, but don't insist on preaching. Some ministers insist on preaching just for the experience of speaking in a foreign country. Preaching should serve the needs of the people on the field, not the preacher.

In cross-cultural ministry, a positive response to a message is often an acceptance of the messenger rather than an understanding or acceptance of the message. Whatever the response, leave the fruit of the ministry in God's hands. Hannah Whitall Smith's reference to an old quotation *(The Christian's Secret of a Happy Life)* is good advice for those who race home with stories of the multitudes that responded to their preaching. "Never indulge, at the close of an action, in any self-reflective acts of any kind, whether of self-congratulation or self-despair. Forget the things that are behind, the moment they are past, leaving them with God."[2]

Be Ready to Give a Reason

Be open to different ways to be used by God. One volunteer retiree couple, who worked in food distribution to the homeless, said, "We never knew what a day would bring. Each morning we got up and said, 'Lord, what do you have in store for us today?'" The couple said that on one occasion, a young migrant couple came to the place where they were staying. The woman was having a miscarriage and they didn't know where to turn for help. The volunteers were able to direct the couple to medical care and to witness to them.

If doors close to planned areas of witnessing, look for God to open other doors. Be open to God's way of using you.

Ask God for a special touch of love and understanding. Some people will be unlovely and ungrateful, and may even try to take advantage of your kindness. Humanly speaking, your response to them will not be *love*. You will want to defend your rights. Only through the Spirit's power can you model love in these situations.

Depend on God for wisdom and power in witnessing. One

couple said, "We weren't bold, but we felt so full of power to talk with people. There was never any stumbling about what to say."

Be ready to give a reason for the hope that you have. The questions most often asked are: "Why? Why are you here? Why are you doing this?" Be ready to tell others why you are helping them but:

- Never point to yourself as a hero.
- Don't give people the impression that you are trying to convert them to *your* beliefs or way of living.
- Tell them what Jesus Christ has done in your life.
- Tell them that Jesus is alive and cares for them.
- Tell them that the power of Christ is available to them, and His power can free them from the bondage of sin.
- Emphasize a new start, not past sins.
- Help people with the changes they are trying to make, instead of the changes you think they should make.
- Rely on the Holy Spirit to enable you to minister. Without His power, our patience and love will soon wear thin. Ask God to help you see people as He sees them.

Ways to Help the Local Pastor and Local Christians

Effective witnessing is not limited to speaking in church services. Sports and music provide opportunities to interact with members of the local congregation on a more informal basis. Joining a soccer game or allowing a musician to join your musical group helps build rapport with the local people, and provides opportunities for personal witness. If time and opportunity permit, visit in homes, share photos of your family, and ask to hear their folk songs. Learn more of the language.

Take time to get acquainted with local pastors and Christian workers. Be sure to listen to their joys, burdens, concerns, and needs. Let them know that you want to work together with them and become a part of their ministry. Encourage and affirm them by sharing insights into God's Word and asking them to share specific prayer requests with you. You may want to correspond with the pastor after you return home.

Dianne and Gene corresponded with a Rwandan pastor and his wife, providing encouragement during the turbulent days preceding the Rwandan civil war. "When I started to write," Dianne said, "I had no idea what to say to someone from another culture. I couldn't talk about working at the office or shopping at the mall. I had to look deep in my own heart, at what God was doing in my life, and rely on Him to direct me in what I wrote." You may feel that you have nothing to say to someone of another culture, but if you look to God for guidance you will find ways to cross cultural barriers and provide encouragement.

Problems with Local Relationships

Problems in regard to team members and local people have occurred most often in the areas of romantic relationships and giving practices.

Women should especially keep in mind that in some countries, declarations of undying love are common; marriage to you means US citizenship.

In some locations, giving out your address to newfound friends is an invitation to trouble. You will be hounded by pleas for funds for schooling, sick children, and burials. Some relatives are buried by every team that passes through the area. Follow the missionary's advice about giving out your address.

Team members are often approached by young people who want to better themselves through education or travel to North America. Often these young people appear to be exceptionally intelligent and motivated. Do not, however, take on sponsorship of an individual until you consult the missionary and church leaders. Sometimes bolder, more charismatic students have shallow commitments to Christian service, while reserved, less aggressive students are deeply committed to ministry. In dealing with young Christian workers who are asking for sponsorship or education abroad keep these things in mind:

- Be careful about raising the hopes of young people.
- Never give any promises of support while on the field.
- Encourage young people to *first* take advantage of educational

opportunities in their own country before pursuing study abroad.

- If you wish to support a particular young person, first consult the missionary and the local pastor. Follow their direction in regard to sponsorship.
- When you return home, follow through on your plans.

Warm Fuzzies

"Members of mission teams have the biggest hearts in the world," a missionary from Africa said. "These people are the most caring, most sacrificial people in the home church."

Team members have literally given the clothes off their backs and shoes from their feet. The generosity of team members, however, has created long-term problems for the missionary and future volunteers.

When the first mission team arrived at the remote town of Temps Perdu, Haiti, the local people worked side-by-side with the team during the day and joined in campfire songs each evening. The relationship was one of mutual work, worship, and play. On the last day, against the request of the missionary, team members began distributing their clothes, shoes, and watches to their new friends.

A month later, when a second team arrived to finish the structure, the team members were besieged by requests for favorite shirts, jeans, shoes, and watches. Not only did the local people refuse to work, but their bidding wars hindered the work of the team members.

The team member who hands out gifts will definitely take home warm fuzzy feelings, but the ongoing cause of missions will be hindered. Some gifts have even caused church divisions. When one team member presented a typewriter to a favorite worker, the church split over whether the typewriter was personal property or church property.

The best type of giving is from one congregation to another congregation. This prevents begging and jealousy.

Giving to Children

Giving to children should be done through organizations such as schools, churches, and orphanages. Give toothbrushes rather than candy. Never hand out candy or money to children on the street or around the church site. This practice encourages begging. If you want to give money to a needy child on the street, have the child shine your shoes or carry a package.

Appropriate Personal Giving

Some personal giving is appropriate. If you eat a meal or stay in a local home, a small gift is appropriate. Token gifts for staff members of a mission guest house, interpreters that travel with the team, and chauffeurs are also appropriate. (Tipping is sometimes expected. Check with the missionary.) A small craft from your home area is an excellent token gift. Also appropriate are small decorative soaps, candles, key chains, paperweights, and small dried flower arrangements.

If the team has been working with one particular pastor, they might want to leave a more substantial gift, such as a donation for personal use or a set of towels.

Some gifts are also appropriate for friends you have made within the local congregation. Gifts that will strengthen bonds of friendship but not create begging or jealousy are photos of you and your family, postcards from your home area, bookmarks, team photos, and photo-calendars. If your church puts out an attractive Scripture calendar, bring some for gifts. These little gifts will mean a lot, even if the words are in English. These gifts emphasize the mutual bond of friendship rather than the division between *have's* and *have not's*.

But You Promised

Indiscriminate handouts are destructive; but equally destructive is the habit of making promises. As one missionary said, "Team members' mouths outrun their pocketbooks." Team members see the enormous needs and make all kinds of promises while they are on the field. As soon as they get home, many people forget their promises. The locals do not forget.

When the photos, the guitar, and the funds for schooling do

not appear, the missionary is accused of lying and theft. **Do not make promises to the local people.** If you decide to donate goods or sponsor students, work through the missionary. Let the missionary inform the recipients *when* donations or funds arrive on the field.

Giving to Beggars

Everyone, including missionaries, struggles with the issue of begging. There really is no set rule for giving to beggars. On the field the missionary can usually advise you as to who has legitimate needs and who does not. In many countries people beg for money then give it to a *boss,* who provides them with a daily salary. The boss is wealthy; the beggars survive. Sometimes parents maim their children in order to use them as beggars. On one occasion, I came out of a store and noticed a blind man and his escort. I mentioned them to my daughter who had been waiting in the car. "I just saw them trade places," she said. "A few minutes ago, the other one was *blind.*"

In Haiti we discouraged team members from giving to the *severely* wounded who needed money for medical attention. Smeared chicken innards and blood created those wounds. We encouraged them to give to an elderly, contorted, gentleman who hobbled through our neighborhood. We asked them not to give to the young girl with a missing hand and foot who begged outside the supermarket. Although missionaries had measured her for prostheses, her parents refused to let her be outfitted.

We advised team members to say no to the mothers who exposed emaciated infants to the tropical sun in order to get money. We knew that loving parents shielded their children from the sun and that these women bore a child each year to use as a begging ploy.

Listen to the missionary's suggestions, but in the end you'll have to decide for yourself about giving to beggars. If you give to someone who approaches you in a crowded area such as a market, airport, or tourist attraction, you may find yourself besieged by beggars. If you give to someone who has a station on the street where they beg daily, you can usually slip a coin to them without being noticed. Always give discreetly.

If you do not give to people who approach you, don't just brush the people aside. Look at them, acknowledge their presence, shake your head, and say, "Not today." For most beggars this approach works. A few will hound you until you get back into your vehicle.

It Is Better to Receive

Four years after the Guatemalan earthquake, five team members who had helped in reconstruction returned to Guatemala. One of the local women invited the visitors to her new home for a meal. "When you were here before," she said. "I had no home and you gave to me. Now, I have my home and I want to give to you."

The team members, however, felt badly because she had spent a weeks pay on the special meal. Before they left, they insisted on paying for the meal. When she objected, they pressed money in her hands and told her to use it for shoes for the children. As the team members drove away, she stood clutching the money and saying, "But I wanted to give to you today."

When you are presented gifts that you know are being given at great sacrifice, graciously accept the gift. You may feel better by refusing the gift, but set aside your own need to feel good. The giver's feelings are more important. Assure the giver that you will treasure and use the gift.

Be careful, however, about admiring an item in someone's home. In some cultures they will feel obligated to present it to you. In all your interaction with local people, ask yourself, "Will this action weaken or develop mutual bonds of respect?"

A Spiritual Work

The role of the effective mission volunteer is far more complex than driving nails or conducting a survey. One pastor said, "Team members should never come with the attitude of 'I'll do my job, and then go home.' Team members should come to do a spiritual work. The volunteers need to come expecting to help someone, and show that person how, in turn, to help someone else."

Effective volunteers will not only exhibit the attitudes of servanthood, openness, and flexibility, but they will inspire others to be mission volunteers.

Session Four
Individual or Group Assignments

Roommates

Take a few minutes to share stories about roommates. What actions irritated or disgusted you? How did you resolve differences? What attitudes created enduring friendships? Discuss what you value in a roommate: Conversation? Silence? Neatness?

Last-Minute Details

1. What logistical problems have you encountered? Do you have necessary documents? Have you found everything on your packing list? How do you plan to carry your money for safekeeping?
2. What hindrances to going are you encountering at home? At work? With finances?
3. Work together to handle all the logistical details ahead of time, so that when departure time comes, you can be more focused on the purpose of the tour—ministry.
4. If packing with others to cut down luggage, double-check to see who is taking what: first-aid kit, blow-dryer, drill, fan, etc.
5. Practice language phrases and a special song.
6. In the material on relationships, what did you find surprising? In what areas do you think you will have the most difficulty practicing servanthood? What misconceptions did you discover in your own thinking concerning missionaries? Nationals?
7. Some veteran volunteers may have differences in opinion regarding field activities and ministry, especially in the area of giving. Discuss these differences openly. As a team, make policy decisions. As an individual volunteer, abide by team decisions.

Take Time to Praise

Take time to share with teammates how God has answered prayer in regard to your going to the mission field. Be sure to include any special Scripture verses that have encouraged you.

Take time to pray for family or friends who may be concerned about the trip. Ask God to give them peace and assurance about your going.

Assignment

Make sure you have transportation and know the exact time and place to meet teammates for departure.

If the team is from a local church and the departure time is reasonable, strengthen church/team bonds by inviting church members to come see the team off. Ask a pastor or layperson to lead a chorus of praise and a prayer for protection. When church members are involved in your departure, they will be eager to hear your experiences when you return.

Personal Prayer

Ask God to give you a calm spirit as you finish preparations and as you travel. As much as possible, start centering your thoughts and prayers on the ministry ahead.

PART FIVE

Return Home

CHAPTER 21

Homeward Bound

Playing Tourist

Mission tours usually provide one or two days for sight-seeing and shopping. If you are visiting a city in an impoverished country, you'll probably want to hire a guide. The guide can help you find items on your shopping list and direct you to local points of interest. Of greater service, the guide will fend off beggars, vendors, and other guides that would otherwise hound you. Two to four team members can use one guide. In developed countries, you won't usually be hassled by vendors and beggars. Also, the fee of a tour guide might be cost prohibitive.

Be aware that some guides may rush you through a market to the stalls and stores of relatives and friends. Don't hesitate to stop and look at items that attract your attention along the way, or ask to be taken to shops other than the ones recommended by the guide.

Bargaining
1. Don't worry about taking advantage of a merchant. They have bottom-line prices, and they won't lose money.
2. Never show a wad of money. Put a few bills in one pocket or a change purse. Make purchases from that pocket and replenish your bargaining pocket between sales.
3. Ask the price, then roughly divide it by half. For example, if the asking price is $20, offer $12.
4. Haggle until you're about halfway between the two prices. For a $20 item, expect to pay around $15.
5. If the merchant won't come down, slowly unroll your tiny wad of money and show that you only have $15. If he won't take it, walk away. He will probably call you back. If he doesn't call you back, and you really want the item, look around a few minutes, then return and pay the merchant's price.

Customs vary from country to country; but for the most part, merchants who sell in stores have set prices. Vendors who sell from open-air stands and flea market-style stalls will bargain with you.

Customs Allowance
In the US, each person is allowed to bring back about $400 worth of duty-free items. This includes gifts to you and those you intend to give to others. Keep a list of what you buy, the price, and all receipts. You can lump small purchases together as miscellaneous items. If you plan to spend over $400, order an information brochure regarding policies. You can obtain it at the nearest customs office or by requesting information from the Consumer Information Center, P. O. Box 100, Pueblo, CO 81002.

Canadian citizens returning to Canada will need to check on Canadian customs regulations.

Collector's Items
In shopping, you'll be tempted to buy a lot of junk souvenirs

---

Suitable Souvenirs

- Additions to a collection—antiques, porcelain figures, animal figurines, stamps, coins, gems, rocks, etc.
- Coffee-table books with photos of the country
- Coats of arms (usually wooden or porcelain plaques)
- Wood carvings
- Paintings or sculptures
- Pottery
- Jewelry
- Music (instruments, tapes, CDs)

---

because they are so colorful and cheap. These are fine for small gifts to friends. If you want an enduring memento, however, or if you travel and collect souvenirs from many countries, you may want to buy one or two more durable souvenirs.

If you plan to speak or write about your experiences, you'll find a map, postcards, travel brochures, and packaged slides will jog your memory and enrich your presentation.

If You Decide to Buy . . .

- **Necklaces** made from seeds. Do not give them to families with small children. Some of the seeds are poisonous.
- **Goat skin rugs** or any other hide. Make sure they are fully tanned. Also make sure the US has no prohibition against hides from that country.
- **Endangered species. Don't!** Do not attempt to bring back furs, ivory, or other items from endangered species.
- **Antiquities.** Be sure that you know the laws and obey the laws when taking antiquities out of the country. Penalties are severe!! Make sure you have a receipt and a certificate of authenticity. In areas of archaeological digs, you will be offered *genuine relics* on the street. These are fresh "antiquities," made daily.
- **Food.** Make sure it is processed, canned, or packaged. Items such as coffee, vanilla, and candy are fine. Some fresh fruits

(pineapple) can be taken out, but you'll have to pass through an agricultural inspection line in US customs. Sugar cane (stick) is usually prohibited. Check with the missionary before taking any fresh fruit. Don't take live plants or animals.

- **Sea creatures.** Don't take anything live from the sea, especially coral. Never, ever, put a live shell in a plastic bag, in your luggage, and take it home. You'll have to throw away the shell, the luggage, and everything that is in the luggage to get rid of the stench—plus, it may be months before your car smells clean again, if ever.

Tying Up Loose Ends

Make sure your tickets have been reconfirmed (usually 72 hours) before departure. The team leader or missionary usually reconfirms tickets for the entire team at one time.

Before leaving, make sure all accounts are settled at your lodging place. Sometimes sodas and stamps are sold on an honor system. Team members often borrow from each other when they can't get change or don't have money for an unplanned expense. Make sure your accounts are settled with team members.

Prepare to keep promises you made. Did you promise to mail packages for the missionary? Phone someone when you return? Make sure you have made the necessary arrangements to carry out these promises.

Do you have the addresses of team members with whom you plan to keep in touch?

Packing for the Return Trip

Tape the lids of liquids (especially vanilla or perfumes) which you have purchased and place the bottles in plastic bags. If you have room, store them upright in your carry-on bag.

If the missionary lives in an area where quality toiletries are expensive or hard to find, you may want to leave some of yours. Items commonly left include: hair spray, shaving cream, lotions, sunscreen, suntan oil, insect repellent, and snacks. If you want to leave clothes to be given away, give them to the missionary to distribute.

When exchanging currency, keep some money in local currency for departure tax.

Prepare Your Document Pouch
Tickets

Passport

Visas

Phone numbers—home, US mission contact, foreign contact

$20 in single bills for tips

Keys to luggage

Pen

Money in local currency for departure tax

Receipts and list of items to declare on customs form

Departure
If you have a badge or some other means of team identification, have it visible when you go to the airport. If the missionary or team leader does not arrange for porters, choose a porter as you did when you arrived. If you are with teammates, you can usually work together to get luggage to the ticket counter. *Don't ever leave any luggage unattended.*

Again, *do not carry packages for strangers.*

Luggage check is similar to that on a domestic flight. Departure tax is paid at the ticket counter when you check your luggage. After checking your luggage, you'll go through immigration. If you plan to do any shopping at the airport, do it before going through immigration. After passing through immigration, you cannot return to the main terminal of the airport.

At immigration, pay attention to signs and stay behind designated lines until you are called. Have your passport and visa in hand. As a rule, your visa is taken by the officer and your passport is stamped *exit.*

US Customs and Immigration
On the plane, you'll be given a customs declaration form. One question concerns being around farm animals. In a country where livestock roams free, it's hard to avoid being around animals. Unless you have been working on a farm, answer *no* to questions

about being on a farm. Place your customs declaration form in your document pouch until you get to customs.

Even though you have a connecting flight, you will go through immigration and customs at the point of reentry into the States. When you enter the airport, signs will direct you to immigration. This is often a lengthy walk. Get your passport out and open it to your photo page. As you near immigration, you may hear "All US citizens with passports to the right," or some other such directions. If the immigration agent seems to be waving people through, hold your open passport beside your face as you pass.

Sometimes the agents will conduct closer examinations of passports, but if you have a current passport, you will have no problem. If you do not have a passport, get out your documents and go to the long, long line for *citizens without passports*.

After passing through immigration put your passport back in your document pouch. As a rule, you won't need your passport again. Proceed to baggage claim and get your luggage. Again, if the team leader has baggage claim tickets, wait until all bags are accounted for before clearing customs. As much as possible, stay with other members of the group when passing through customs. Before entering the customs lane, have declaration form in hand and keys to luggage. Place everything, including purses, on the counter or belt. The agent may ask where you've been and why you traveled. Answer questions briefly. Open the bags the agent requests. Usually, the agent then stamps your declaration form and gives it back to you. Another agent will take the form from you at the customs exit. Once outside the customs door, you will proceed as with any domestic flight. If your connection is close or your luggage is too heavy, get a porter to handle your luggage. It may cost you a few dollars, but it's worth getting to a flight on time.

If you have live plants, fruits, or vegetables you'll need to go through an agricultural clearance line.

Debrief

Some tours, especially those geared to teens or young adults, include a day or two of debriefing. Adult tours may only have an hour of debriefing. If the tour does not provide debriefing, set aside some time to evaluate your experience. If you know that when you arrive home you'll have to *hit the ground running* in order to catch up on business, and that you will have to return to a full work schedule immediately, take time on the plane to assess your trip. Be honest with yourself. Include both good and bad experiences. You may want to do this together with another team member. To help you evaluate your experience, use the Debriefing Material in Session Six at the end of chapter 22.

The Yo-Yo Syndrome

When you return home, expect to encounter some physical exhaustion and emotional yo-yoing. You've been operating with your senses on full-open for several days. You've been absorbing new sights, sounds, smells, tastes, and ideas on a nonstop basis. You've been meeting new people daily and have probably conversed more than usual. Add to these drastic changes in routine and the stress of staying in strange, cramped, living quarters. Your body and senses are ready for a rest. Don't be surprised if you feel physically beat or your emotions plunge.

If your schedule allows it, take a couple of days to relax when you get home. Let your body readjust to your home climate, food, and water. Take time to unwind with your family.

Reverse Culture Shock

If you've been in a very poor country, expect to go through reverse culture shock when you reenter your own culture. It can be more emotionally distressing than the shock of entering a new culture.

After living in an impoverished nation, you will return home to take pleasure in smooth roads, the abundance of food, hot showers, and your climate-controlled home. At the same time, you will feel resentment that your own nation wastes so much and spends so much on nonessentials while others are dying from lack of pure water, food, and basic medical care.

One woman was so happy to get back to her clean modern kitchen that she kissed the kitchen floor; a few minutes later she was crying. Her cabinets overflowed with junk food, while children she had just left were dying from lack of food. Your emotions will yo-yo. You'll be happy and yet angry. During these first days back, be careful about venting your feelings unless it's to someone who has visited or lived in other countries.

Don't give a full mission presentation the week you arrive home. Limit any public comments to a short testimony. Later, when you're more rested, when your emotions have stabilized, and when you have had time to evaluate your experience as a whole, give a mission presentation.

What's Wrong with Me?

Be sure to continue your malaria medication according to the doctor's instructions (usually 4 to 6 weeks after your return). Malaria medicine does not prevent infection, but suppresses the multiplication of parasites in the liver. Keep taking malaria medicine as instructed. Stopping the medication too soon may allow the parasites to multiply. The resulting full-blown malaria will be more resistant to medication.

If you have been drinking purified water for two weeks or more, you may experience some gastrointestinal discomfort when you go back to your water at home. This should disappear within a couple of days.

If, however, during the next six months, you experience any extreme exhaustion, fever, or illness which cannot be identified, be sure to tell your doctor which country you visited. Unless your doctor is acquainted with tropical diseases, malaria symptoms will be mistaken for the flu. The fatality rate for malaria is higher in countries where malaria is not found because doctors do not recognize it. If symptoms of malaria persist, insist on a blood test to rule out malaria.

Ciguatera toxic poisoning (from fish) is seldom recognized in North America and there is really no way to diagnose it except by symptoms. Sometimes people forget that they ate fish because the bizarre symptoms develop several days after eating the meal. If you ate fish in a tropical reef area and experienced vomiting or diarrhea (even mild), then several days later developed bizarre symptoms such as visual disturbances, toothache, or reversal of sensitivity to heat or cold, suspect ciguatera.

The greatest problem with ciguatera is not in the illness itself but in diagnosis. People feel so exhausted they are sure they have a deadly disease. Tropical doctors will recognize the problem immediately. North American doctors will turn you inside out and empty your bank account and never discover the problem. If your doctor can't seem to pinpoint any reason for your extreme exhaustion and you experienced any of the bizarre symptoms, plus you remember eating fish (including airline meals), ask your doctor if it could be ciguatera. If it is, readjust your schedule and pace until you feel better. There isn't any treatment. Strong symptoms may persist for a year, but they will gradually diminish.

If persistent stomach or intestinal problems develop even after you've been home several months, ask the doctor to test for parasites or amoebas.

CHAPTER 22

Home Sweet Home

What a Waste

Volunteers often hear, "Why did you spend all that money for the trip? Wouldn't it have been better to just send the money? Wasn't that a waste of money?"

One volunteer who served in Brazil said, "It's hard to explain to people what a mission trip does to you. You come back so different. You feel related to missions. When a missionary comes to your home church, you hang onto every word.

"You appreciate your own country more," he continued. "In other countries, people struggle to survive. They will walk for days to attend a service and stay all day. You don't see that interest in the gospel here. When you come home, you feel disappointed that others take so much for granted."

When you return to your home church you may struggle with

conflicting emotions concerning your church's priorities. On the field you may have seen hundreds jammed into a tin-roofed, one-room church with backless pews. Many in the congregation may have walked several hours on muddy trails in order to attend services.

At home, your air-conditioned, carpeted to match the padded-pews church may be raising thousands of dollars to build a covered drive-through so that parishioners can be dropped at the church door instead of walking across the parking lot.

You may feel angry and disappointed when your enthusiasm for missions is met with polite nods and "excuse me, I have to catch someone before he leaves."

If you cannot tell your mission experience to others, you can still use the knowledge you gained on the field to make a difference in your home church and culture. As you try to put the lessons you learned on the field into practice, remember:

1. The realities of your own culture—in your culture, comfort and convenience are important. Ours is a materialistic society.
2. You have had the privilege of visiting another culture where relationships may have been more important than possessions.
3. Instead of focusing on the material excesses of our culture, focus on improving and building relationships with others.
4. As you build relationships, you will find ways to communicate your mission experiences and concerns.

Turn Off Attitudes

- Don't exalt yourself as an authority on missions.
- Don't act *holier than thou* because you've been on the mission field.
- Don't go around depressed because of the condition of the people on the mission field. Rather, focus on the positive things you learned from the culture.
- Don't get impatient when people don't respond to your vision for missions. Allow time for people to catch a glimpse of what you saw. Your changed life will be the greatest testimony.

5. Avoid *turn off attitudes*. Poor attitudes will adversely affect
   future support of any mission projects you advocate or mission
   trips you undertake.

This Is a Picture Of . . .

On a grueling deputation schedule, a missionary couple was scheduled to make a six-hour driving detour to speak at a Michigan church.

When they arrived to find only 12 people in attendance, they
were disappointed that the long drive had resulted in such a small
turnout. A man who had taken several trips to the mission field
was in charge. He started the service by saying he would like to
tell about the trip he had taken to the Dominican Republic the previous winter.

"I haven't had time," he said, "to check these slides or put
them in any kind of order, but I know you'll want to see them all."

During the next 90 minutes he showed slides. He showed dark
ones and bleached ones. He moved the projector to project postage
stamp-size images, and to project images that covered the screen
and curtains behind the screen. When one slide was in sideways, he
picked up the projector, and turned it sideways. The projector light
both illuminated the slide and spotlighted the missionaries sitting
nearby. He narrated the slides by saying, "Let me see if I can remember what this is. Oh, yes, this is a picture of . . ."

By 8:45 P.M. everyone was yawning. The volunteer finally
said, "That's all I have about my trip, but we have a missionary
couple here who are getting ready to go to the Dominican
Republic." Turning to the missionaries, he said, "Do you have anything you want to say?"

Since everyone was clearly bored and the hour was late, the
missionary limited his comments to 15 minutes. As soon as he sat
down, the volunteer said to the missionary, "Now, we're going
down to the Dominican Republic to help you next spring. I'm getting up a team right now." For the next half-hour the volunteer
explained what he intended to do on the field and how he was
going to conduct the tour. Finally, he closed by assuring the missionary that he would definitely be there to help in a few months.

The following suggestions will help you avoid many of the mistakes made by this eager volunteer.

Team Presentations

In presenting a missions program in a church, use as many members of the team as possible. If members come from different churches in a local area, put together a program, then present the program in each of your churches.

Use variety and creativity. For example, use an interview format in which a leader questions each team member about a specific aspect of the tour.

Set up a curio table with souvenirs team members brought home. Label exhibits. Have a team member at the display to explain the importance of items.

Make a display board with the best photos. If necessary, use some postcards. Label all photos. Have a team member at the display to answer questions.

Use music. Play the music of the country you visited preceding and following the service. Sing a chorus in the language of that country. Also use the music for background in slide or video presentations.

Be available to answer questions at the end of the presentation.

Contents of Presentation

- Avoid hearsay. Stick with facts. Hearsay may be more dramatic, but it isn't always accurate. Before you state, "children are sacrificed," make sure the information comes from a reliable source.
- Give a balanced view, by sharing both your failures and your successes.
- Avoid humor that degrades the country you visited. Your audience may include expatriates from that country.
- Talk about what you have learned from God and miracles you have witnessed, giving God the glory for it all.
- Thank your family and friends. Let them know that what was accomplished would not have been possible without their support.
- Emphasize the needs of missionaries and others on the field. Be specific.

Slide Shows

- Choose a few of the very best lighted slides. Arrange them in order to focus on a particular theme or aspect of the mission tour.
- In presenting slides, write a script and illustrate it with slides. Avoid "and this is a picture of . . ." Tape the script and play it during the presentation.
- Check out the lighting in the church. Don't show slides in the morning or late afternoon, unless you can darken the room.
- Never show an unedited video in a public presentation. Bore your family and friends, but not a general audience.

Avoid

- Generalizations (Your encounter with one police officer who wanted a bribe is not a portrayal of all residents of the country.)
- Travelogues or lists of places and people
- Emotional pleas to gain pity or impose guilt
- Inside jokes
- Course or vulgar references
- Telling all (In a public presentation, leave out gory details and life-threatening situations.)
- Being a martyr (Tell close friends about being eaten by bedbugs, but leave it out of public presentations.)

Don't be discouraged if the response is lukewarm. One man spoke of attending a missionary service with around 300 other people. "As far as I know," he said, "I was the only one who responded to the call for volunteers, but that day changed my life." He not only traveled to a foreign field, but helped raise teams and funds for other projects.

Keeping the Vision Alive

Be sure to participate in team presentations, but don't limit sharing your mission experience to team programs. There are many opportunities for individual volunteers to share their mission experience. In each situation, slant your presentation to catch the attention of your audience.

- Large church. If your church is large, approach different groups within the church: senior adults, youth, children, women, men, etc.
- Christian schools. Many Christian schools seek chapel speakers.
- Local newspaper. If you have writing skills, write an article and present it with photos, or contact the paper and let them know you could give an interview. Follow the same rules as in presenting a public program. Be sure to stick to facts.
- Civic clubs. In these presentations you may want to focus more on travelogue or the cultural aspects of the country and close with an anecdote that illustrates a spiritual truth.
- Newsletter. Share your experience in a newsletter to friends or family who cannot attend one of your presentations. Include photos.
- Letters to team members. Keep the mission field experience alive by keeping in touch with fellow team members. Plan a get-together after a few months, a year, and five years.

Effective Linking

Effective linking of the mission field and the home church, however, will not occur unless you get past reliving the experience and set goals for future involvement. Set short-range and long-range goals, but don't set goals that you can't reach. Also, set local goals and foreign field goals.

To start, ask yourself, "What am I personally responsible to do?"

If you made promises to anyone on the field, you have a responsibility to carry out those promises. Take definite steps to fulfill the need. If there is a delay, write to explain that you are still working on the need. If you find you cannot keep the promises you made, be sure to write to the individual and explain. Someone else may be able to meet the need. If the promise involves a national who is working closely with a missionary, write to the missionary also and explain the situation. This way, if there are any questions, the missionary may be able to help.

If you mentioned a *possibility* to someone, immediately determine if you will be able to provide the need. Keep the person updated at all times on how the project is going. Don't be afraid to say, "I tried, but just couldn't swing it."

Your next step in mission involvement should be with your local missions committee. Let the missions leaders know that you are interested and willing to help. Volunteer to help with missionary conferences, banquets, or mission emphasis promotions and education.

Other ways that individual volunteers can promote missions include:

* Teaching a small group with a missions emphasis, or teaching in a missions education program or organization;
* Teaching a Sunday School class with a missions emphasis;
* Helping other volunteers obtain funds for mission trips;
* Helping in orientation and preparation of other teams;
* Giving to mission projects;
* Hosting a missionary family;
* Assisting a refugee family;
* Inviting an international student to your home.

How You Can Help on the Field

Some team members come home so moved by their experience that they decide to return. **Do not return on your own.** Don't write to missionaries asking for a job. No matter how skilled you may be, do not go to the field to help a missionary without a specific invitation that clearly spells out your job and the provision for your housing and food.

One group of dentists appeared at a mission clinic ready to do dental work. They were irate when the missionaries told them their room and board would be $3.25 a day. The dentists said, "We've flown here at our own expense and you're charging us to work for you." The missionaries, however, had a limited budget. The team's need for water for laundry, showers, clinic work, and other needs required extra (very expensive) fuel for the generator. Since the food supplies were not adequate to feed the men for ten

Writing to Missionaries

- Share what God is doing in your life and Scriptures that have encouraged you.
- Send funny friendship cards. Clip jokes and cartoons that you think would appeal to the missionary.
- Be creative in your writing. Write to all members of the family. When our daughter was a teenager and living in Haiti, a Sunday School teacher in Pennsylvania wrote her periodically. Although he was old enough to be her grandfather, she looked forward to his letters. One letter that impressed her was simply a description of a snowfall and the birds and rabbits that he could see from his window. No matter your age or the ages of the missionaries, you can find creative ways to lift their spirits.
- If the missionary is acquainted with members of your family, include news about them. Do not, however, give a newsletter account of every child and grandchild's accomplishments. Relate family news that would be of particular interest to the missionary.
- Do give them news about your church, but avoid gossip.
- Send clippings and articles concerning their hobbies or special interests.
- Don't expect immediate responses to your letters. On the mission field, letter writing often comes last on the schedule.

days, the missionary had to make a three-day trip to the city (more expensive fuel) for additional supplies.

Some team members have found national pastors more eager to accept their help than missionaries. If you get approval from a national pastor to come and help, **do not expect free food, board, and transportation.** In many countries, providing food and lodging for a volunteer would place serious financial strains on the local pastor, his family, and the congregation.

The emphasis cannot be made strongly enough—**do not return to help missionaries or national workers unless you**

go through the proper channels and have total provision for your expenses arranged ahead of time.

There are better ways for volunteers to help the missionary than returning to the field.

- Give financially. Help support missionaries by giving on a regular basis to missions.
- Give financially to special projects. Contact the missionary or mission board about projects to which you could give. Do not decide on your own what the missionary or national church needs. Ask them.
- Cultivate friendships with missionaries. Write to a missionary. (See sidebar Writing to Missionaries on previous page.)
- Phone them. Ask ahead about what days or hours would be most convenient for phone calls. Keep in mind time zones.
- If the missionary has parents or children in your area, get in touch with them. See if you can help them.
- Help the local church in making hospitality arrangements for visiting missionaries.
- Open your home to missionaries. Let them know that if they are in your area, your door is open.

How to Host a Missionary Family

When missionaries return home, they often run into many problems relating to travel, housing, and adjustment to their home culture. Often, they have no idea where to turn for help. Volunteers can really make a difference in that transition period.

When our car broke down on the interstate outside of Atlanta, a team member had our car towed to his mechanic and took us home for a relaxing meal and pleasant private accommodations. That same evening another volunteer who lived nearby invited us to his home. There, he showed us pictures of his prize-winning Tennessee Walkers. Then, he turned the lights on the riding track and allowed our teenage daughter to ride one of his prize horses.

When political instability in Haiti forced us to return to the States for an indeterminate time, one family offered their vacation home to us. Another provided a vehicle. When we returned home to stay, a volunteer handed us the keys to a truck and travel trailer and told us to take a much needed vacation.

If the missionary stays in your home, be sure to provide private accommodations. After a night on the living room sofa bed and listening to your dog slurp water and kick fleas, the missionary may feel like a part of your family, but the missionary will not go away rested.

Also, if the missionary is going from one extreme climate to another, either adjust your thermostat or loan him clothes to make his stay more comfortable.

If you serve on a missions committee, you may want to suggest providing motel accommodations for the missionary. Although my husband and I enjoyed the hospitality of many families, we were elated when one church put us in a motel. That Saturday night we ordered pizza and watched a basketball game on TV. The next morning, the missions committee chairman and his wife met us for breakfast, and we had a delightful time getting acquainted before the morning church service. The missions committee had provided both fellowship and a very much needed evening of relaxation.

When a missionary is on furlough, expenses run much higher than on the field. Clothes, birthday and Christmas gifts, equipment, and supplies for the next term must be purchased in order to take them back as accompanied (customs-free) baggage. The missionary's budget may include entertainment expenses, but use of those funds has probably been planned by the family in advance. They may go for a vacation to see relatives or a day at Sea World. There will be little room for unplanned entertainment expenses.

If you have the funds or can get free tickets, invite them to attend concerts, plays, professional sports, or tourist attractions. Make it clear that they will go as your guests and you will provide the tickets.

If your budget doesn't allow it, opt for free or lower expense entertainment that would be within the missionary's budget such as a day at the beach, museums, or concerts in the park. After being out of the country, the missionary family will probably enjoy traditional holiday celebrations: parades, fireworks, caroling, egg hunts, etc.

When you were a volunteer on the mission field, you saw how the missionary family lived. Now, let them see how you live. Invite them to join you. Go fishing, have a picnic, invite friends over for a cookout and a volleyball game. Have fun.

When I was a child, a missionary came to our home. At 5:30 P.M. I turned on the TV to watch *The Little Rascals*. Our family always watched that program at 5:30. My mother, not sure how the missionary felt about *worldly entertainment,* told me to turn off the TV.

"Don't turn it off for me," the missionary said. "It looks like a funny show." I can still remember the feeling of camaraderie with the missionary, as he laughed with us at *The Little Rascals*. Don't put on spiritual airs, just invite the missionaries to join you in your normal family activities and recreation.

If you can afford it, you may want to take members of the missionary family on a shopping trip. If they are just beginning a speaking tour, they will probably need a more updated wardrobe. Offer to buy a suit or a dress. Guide them to the racks within your price range and tell them to make a choice.

If a missionary takes a furlough or resettles in your area, you can be of great help in resettlement. Be specific in asking how you can help with transportation, medical care, education, housing, or employment.

Volunteers who serve through home church channels will do more to help the missionary than volunteers who appear on the field, uninvited, to give the missionary a hand.

Effective volunteers are servants at home as well as on the foreign field. These volunteers do not seek personal fulfillment, but rather the best interests of global missions. They fill a place in missions that no one else can fill. **They are the links that unite the home church and the mission field.**

Session Five
Individual or Group Assignments

Field Exercises

During your stay on the mission field, take time to make the following observations. Log your conclusions in your journal, and if appropriate, share them with teammates during discussion times.

1. Watch to see how God is using each person on the team to meet specific needs. Who is the encourager? Who keeps everyone on a positive note? Who is good with children? Who is good with the youth? How is God using you?

2. Watch for ways to encourage teammates, the missionary, and local church leaders. What characteristic do you admire most in them? Patience? Hard work? Calm attitude? Spiritual depth? What deed of kindness went undetected by others? Take time to let others know that you noticed their servant spirit. What predominant characteristic do you think teammates notice in you?

3. How is God working in your life? How has He encouraged you? Guided you? Rebuked you? What Scripture verses are especially meaningful to you right now? *Daily,* look for evidence that God is at work.

4. How has your view of God and His relationship to the whole world changed? Where do you see the center of God's kingdom now? Is your own country the hub around which God's plan revolves?

5. If your tour is in an underdeveloped nation, watch for similarities in that culture to the historical Bible culture. In many countries, travel by sea and by land will be similar to that of New Testament times. Farming, fishing, food preparation, laundry, construction, and home life may be similar. Recognition of these similarities will enrich your Bible study for the rest of your life.

6. Concerning the foreign culture:
   - What fascinates you?
   - What breaks your heart?
   - What inspires you?

- What makes you angry?
- If you could make one change, what would that be?

7. What positive influences do you see in this culture that your own culture lacks?

Session Six

Individual or Group Assignments

Debriefing Material

1. Surprises. What surprised you about teammates? The culture? The missionaries? The local Christians?

2. Values. How has the experience affected your relationship to your possessions, friends, and God? Have you shifted any priorities?

3. Involvement. How has the experience affected future plans for involvement in your home church?

4. God. In what ways did you see God move in the lives of others? In your life?

5. Disappointment. What was your greatest disappointment?

6. Joy. What was your most enjoyable experience?

7. Changes. What would you do differently on another trip?

8. Return. Do you plan to take another mission tour? Would you change the location or type of tour? If so, how? Overall, was the experience disappointing or satisfying? Would you encourage others to take a mission tour?

9. The call. What would your initial reaction be if you felt God leading you to full-time foreign mission service?

PART SIX

Disaster Assistance

CHAPTER 23

Ministering in the Midst of Disaster

Unless you have personally witnessed or worked in a major disaster you cannot comprehend the resulting chaos. Life as we know it ceases. Safe water, food, electricity, and communications are nonexistent. Without shelter, people are vulnerable to the elements, additional injury, and crime. All that is familiar vanishes: landmarks, businesses, schools, churches, and homes. Many victims go into shock. Some never recover.

Detailed, advance, logistical preparation is vital for working in major disaster areas. **Never throw on a backpack or load up your pickup and head into a major disaster area.** Take time to make adequate preparations before going. Those preparations will depend on the extent of the damage and the time that has elapsed since the initial disaster.

Work Through an Organization

You may go as part of a local team or join volunteers who are already in the disaster area, but **always work through an organization** that has experience with disaster relief. Many denominations have such programs. Working through organizations prevents overlapping assistance, gets to people who would be missed, and increases efficiency. Through trial and error, these organizations have learned how to provide maximum assistance with minimum help and funding.

Following Hurricane Andrew, one organization pulled building permits, one made cabinets, another distributed clothing. Working together, they were able to accomplish much more than working alone. Give up your right to find a devastated family and be their personal hero. Give up the right to show off photos of the roof you singlehandedly nailed down in three days. Work with others in order to accomplish greater good for everyone.

No set of guidelines can be inclusive for every disaster. Each situation requires some special preparation. As time elapses, and the disaster is more manageable, camps for relief workers will be in operation. These camps provide meals and a place to sleep. Be sure you know what will be provided before leaving home.

The following basic guidelines are given for the first month following a major disaster such as Hurricane Andrew. They are listed with the assumption that you have transportation and room to take what you need. Using the following guidelines, adjust your preparation according to the type and extent of the disaster and the time elapsed since the disaster.

Camping and Cooking

Don't expect anyone to take care of you, even if you are with a major organization. Plan to be self-sustained. This means taking water, food, and shelter. Take a tent or some type of camping accommodations. If you need power for a recreational vehicle or camper, take a generator. Don't expect electricity. In hot, humid climates, avoid air mattresses and sleeping bags. Sheets and a 4-inch-thick foam pad will be better. Foam pads are especially comfortable if you're in a dorm-type facility and must sleep on the floor. In dorm-type facilities be sure to take modest sleepwear and flip-flops for moldy showers.

Be prepared to cook your own meals. You will need to take a grill or camp stove. Be sure to stock up on cooking fuels such as propane or charcoal before coming. You won't be able to find them in the disaster area.

Having no electricity often means no running water, so take disposable cooking and eating utensils. Use disposable aluminum pans or heavy foil for cooking. Also use paper plates and napkins, plastic cups, knives, forks, and spoons. **Be sure to include a hand-crank can opener.**

Take plenty of water. Allow one gallon of water, per person, per day. If you're doing construction work in a hot climate, you may want to allow more. For emergency purification put eight drops of bleach in a gallon of water. Take regular bleach—no additives.

Emergency Food List

Beverages (powdered, canned, or packaged fruit juices, instant coffee, tea)

Canned vegetables and fruits

Canned meats (beef, tuna, chicken)

Prepared foods (soups, spaghetti)

Canned beans

Dried fruit

Instant puddings

Powdered milk

Processed cheese or cans of cheese (nonrefrigerated)

Sugar, salt, pepper, seasonings

Onions, garlic, vinegar to help season foods

Crackers (bread will mold quickly in hot, humid climates)

Snacks (crackers, cookies, hard candy)

Snack spreads (peanut butter, cheese spreads, jelly)

Please, Feed the Animals

If you can afford it, take a couple of bags of dry dog and cat food. Following Hurricane Andrew, lost pets roamed the streets looking for food. You may want to put out food for some pets so they'll survive until they're reunited with owners or picked up by animal control.

Don't Plan on Shopping

In deciding what to take, make sure you have what you'll need for the duration of your stay. Stores will be in shambles, supplies gone. Traffic will be gridlocked. Don't expect to run to the corner drugstore for aspirin. (For packing suggestions, read Packing Checklist at the end of chapter 10). Unless you have a generator don't take anything that requires electricity (radios, lights, razors). Use the Emergency Food List for grocery shopping. The items on this list are chosen because they don't need refrigeration and are easy to prepare.

Clothing

You'll need sturdy work shoes to avoid puncture wounds and twisted ankles when walking over debris. The most common injury is due to wearing sneakers instead of sturdy work shoes. Choose a high-top boot for working in flood areas.

Dress for comfort, but dress modestly. Don't plan to do any washing. If there is a laundry, it will be crowded. Take a couple of pairs of work gloves.

Dust is often a major problem following earthquakes. Take disposable face masks if you anticipate a dusty environment. Bandannas can also serve as mouth and nose filters. To keep cool in hot humid areas, dip bandannas in water and wear as a headband.

Other Essentials
- Battery-powered radio (Relief information is broadcast daily.)
- Flashlight/extra batteries
- Lantern (gas or battery)

- Mosquito repellent
- Sunscreen/hats
- Prescription drugs (Take extra prescription drugs in case you decide to extend your stay.)
- Over-the-counter remedies or prescriptions for sinus headaches and allergies
- Toilet tissue
- Container of premoistened towelettes (Try the washcloth-size baby wipes.)
- First-aid kit (Prepare for cuts. Include tweezers to pull splinters, eyedrops, and sore throat medications.)
- Pocket-size first-aid kit (Include antiseptic spray, antibiotic cream, and adhesive bandages in a sealable plastic bag.)
- Contact lens wearers should take prescription glasses in case they work in dusty conditions.
- Clock (battery or windup)
- Matches
- Trash bags
- Fan (If you have a power supply, a fan will make your stay a little more pleasant.)

Garage Sale Items

Don't take clothing or other items to give away unless you have clearance from a relief agency. During the first days following a disaster, all efforts are geared toward distributing water, food, diapers, and the essentials for survival. Other donated items may ruin in the rain due to lack of distribution facilities and personnel. Before taking or sending miscellaneous items, give disaster directors time to meet crucial needs and organize the relief. Then, give your items to the organization that is meeting that particular need. *Make sure any donated clothing is appropriate for the climate.*

Food Donations

For suggested food donations, consult the Emergency Food List. Add to this list: Baby formula, baby food, diapers, sanitary napkins, toilet paper, bath soap, dish and laundry detergent, paper plates, and basic toiletries.

Tools

If you plan to help in reconstruction, take equipment relating to the disaster. For floods you'll need flat shovels, buckets, mops, rags. After tornadoes or hurricanes, you'll need chain saws, rakes, brooms, and containers to hold debris. Following earthquakes you'll need shovels, crowbars, and picks. For all disasters, take a basic tool set with hammer, pliers, socket set, and screwdrivers. Also take an electrical tester and a fire extinguisher.

As time progresses, the needs will change. During massive re-roofing efforts following hurricanes, a large magnet on wheels is great for picking up nails.

Tarps and Plastic Covering

Take a few rolls of *heavy-duty* plastic (lightweight rips too easily), staple gun, and lath strips. Following any disaster you can cover a leaking roof, gaping wall, or door frame and create a shelter for yourself and others. Heavy-duty plastic has many other uses also.

Miscellaneous

Be sure your tetanus shot is up-to-date.

If at all possible, take a generator and extension cords. Take fuel, oil, spare parts, and tools to fix it if necessary. Be able to secure the generator.

Take a good spare tire for all vehicles or trailers and a tire pump. Punctures are common because of debris.

Do not take children. It's difficult enough to work under chaotic conditions without looking out for children.

Take cash. Don't plan on using automated teller machines, credit cards, or traveler's checks. Any banks that open will be swamped; computer systems will be down. Expect to pay at least double for any item you buy.

Lock valuables in your vehicle. Unless the relief organization has a safe place to keep money and valuables, the safest place for them is in your vehicle. To be safe, don't take what you can't keep an eye on or afford to lose. Consider a money belt for keeping cash.

Volunteers do not need guns. Avoid danger; don't confront it. Obey curfews and stay in the area where you are supposed to work. Avoid sight-seeing excursions at night. Avoid high-crime areas at all times.

Take extra gas cans if you're going to be using generators or using fuel for equipment.

Identify Yourself

Before leaving, contact the organization with which you plan to work. Ask for a vehicle decal and personal identification that identifies you as part of the relief effort. If you can't get proper ID before leaving, get it when you check in at the disaster site. Identification with a recognized relief organization will eliminate many hassles. Often, only authorized personnel are allowed to enter disaster areas. You'll find that proper vehicle identification will take you through military and police roadblocks and often eliminate tolls on bridges and turnpikes in the area.

Personal identification is equally important. Looters and con artists descend on disaster areas like vultures. Many home owners guard their property with guns. The people will respond to your offers of help much more heartily if they see you wearing photo identification that connects you to a familiar denomination or a reputable relief agency.

Fifty-Mile Rendezvous

Before entering the disaster area, (30 to 50 miles away, depending on size of disaster) stop to refuel, fill extra gas cans, and fill ice chests. Make final food or supply purchases now. Be sure you have cooking fuels: propane, charcoal, etc. If you get any closer, you'll have difficulty finding supplies. Limit perishables to what can be used in a few days. Don't plan on finding ice in the disaster area. If available, buy a detailed map of the disaster area. If you plan to meet any friends coming from different areas, meet them at this location. Inside the disaster area, traffic, lack of communication, and general chaos will make it difficult to find others. Vehicles in caravans should be equipped with CB radios.

Stop! Before Dark

Do not enter a disaster area for the first time at night, even if you have a map and you are familiar with the area. Curfews, looters, missing street signs, and blocked streets will make your intended destination impossible to reach. Even residents have difficulty locating their homes in the daylight after major disasters.

Safety Tips

1. Always be aware that you are in an unfamiliar and abnormal situation.
2. **Don't drink the water.** Flood surges, broken water mains, and flooded sewage disposal plants will contaminate the local water supply.
3. In any type of disaster, always look out for live electrical wires, pockets of natural gas, fuel spills, and unseen dangers under piles of debris and under flooded areas.
4. Always work in teams, never less than two people together.
5. Never go into a damaged or flooded building with a lantern or open flame of any kind; use a flashlight.
6. In flooded areas, look for electrical outlets that may be underwater, wires that go to a sump pump, water pump, furnace, etc., or extension cords that may have fallen into the water.
7. The first person to go into a flooded basement should be secured with a safety rope held by a second person. Uneven surfaces and hidden objects present a hazard.
8. In a windstorm or earthquake, the same potential hazards exist, but also include hanging or unbalanced objects, limbs on trees, objects supporting each other, and walls that may be structurally damaged.
9. **If a building has shifted on its foundation, use extreme caution.**
10. To avoid being mistaken for a looter or intruder, never enter any house or building unless you have been invited or instructed to do so.[1]

Don't plan to call home. Even if communication lines are restored, there will be long waits at temporary phones, and the lines will be jammed by callers trying to reach relatives and friends.

Secure Generators

Be sure to secure your generator. They sell for a high premium in disaster areas. Following Hurricane Andrew, one couple was watching TV in their RV when the generator stopped running. Thinking the generator had run out of fuel, the owner went outside to refuel it. It was gone. Stolen.

Job Description

Your first reaction to a major disaster will probably be overwhelming disbelief. You will see so much to do and feel inadequate to make a difference. Don't let the immensity of the situation overwhelm you.

Report to the team leader. Describe what you came prepared to do, but express your willingness to do what is most important at that time.

Shortly after Hurricane Andrew struck, a group of volunteers went to Homestead, Florida, to put on roofs. In the early days of the disaster, the main concern was to cover homes with plastic to prevent further damage and remove trees that lay across houses or blocked entryways. When those volunteers were asked to cut and remove trees, they left. "We came to do roofing," they said.

Immediately following a disaster, victims are looking for any type of comfort and help you can provide. Don't limit your assistance to what you came prepared to do. Jump in and do what needs to be done at that moment.

Try to accomplish assigned tasks. There will be so many needs and so many people asking for help, that it will be hard to stay focused and complete one job. Don't be afraid, however, to occasionally abandon the schedule. If a neighbor asks for a helping hand, give a few minutes of time. Don't get locked into a program. You are there to serve others. Do what will be best for the people.

Avoid descending on a situation and taking over. If your exact assignment has not been determined ahead of time, take time to look over the situation with the owners and list the repairs they consider important. The first job is usually protection against further damage by rain and wind. Keep your eyes open for opportunities to help. One crew that went to replace a roof also raked and mowed yards.

Working with Disaster Victims

1. Try to put yourself in the shoes of the disaster victim. Recognize that being on the receiving end of things is not easy. If possible, help the people to help themselves, rather than doing it for them. This gives a sense of personal strength and accomplishment which they need.

2. Be a sensitive listener. This is as important as working. If people want to talk about the disaster and all of the personal details of the tragedy, listen and encourage them to express their feelings. Never probe, however, for accounts of the disaster. Some will be so overwhelmed that they won't be able to discuss it.

3. Recognize all feelings are real and need to be accepted as normal reactions to stress. The following are recognizable, predictable reactions of direct victims: fear and anxiety, being overwhelmed, feeling life is no longer worthwhile, and fear that disaster will recur.

4. Understand the grief of losing possessions. Possessions such as a family heirloom, photo albums, or a house which the owner remodeled are not merely possessions. They are a part of the person.

5. Don't be afraid to reach out. A physical touch (hand on the shoulder, a squeeze on the arm, a hug) is often a good way to say, *I care.*

6. Be particularly sensitive to care for the elderly and children under eight years of age.

7. Affirm people by noticing their courage and telling them what strengths you see.[2]

In Shock

Some volunteers have been upset when they worked in the sun and the owner of the house sat in the shade drinking beer. Keep in mind that you are dealing with traumatized individuals. They may seem disinterested in what you are saying or have vacant stares. Several months after a disaster, many people will still be in shock and denial. Some lose interest in life and never recover.

Completion of a project is not the main goal of the volunteer. One veteran leader of disaster relief said, "Don't look at the project as the goal. The goal is getting in touch with people to whom you can minister. The project enables you to touch these people."

Last Days

As time elapses following the initial disaster, the problems will change. Initially, the problems are with logistics: getting food, water, materials, and shelter to people. In the early stages, everyone pulls together to survive. In the latter stages of reconstruction following a disaster, volunteers will face different problems.

1. People are more impatient, more demanding. Eighteen months without a home will shorten anyone's temper.
2. People may be reluctant to talk about events of the catastrophe. They are talked out. Don't probe or ask them to recount an earthquake or hurricane story.
3. During the first months, some local and federal regulations are suspended in order to get through the crisis. Later, these regulations are reinstated and volunteer teams may be closely monitored.
4. Local people, especially builders, may resent your presence. Although you may be dealing with uninsured or underinsured people who could never hire a contractor, you may be accused of taking jobs and harming the local economy.
5. Relief agencies who cooperated at first may be criticizing each other's work later.

In these situations, show kindness to the victims, regardless of their attitudes. If the work you had planned to do is delayed because of legal hassles, find something else to do. If doors shut to one opportunity, they will open to another. Look for how God is wanting to use you. Do not get involved in government and relief agency conflicts. Let the leaders of the organizations sort out the technicalities and the problems.

It Could Be Me

As a volunteer, you may also suffer some emotional upheaval. Witnessing a major disaster makes you realize that we are all vulnerable to tragedy. None of us is exempt. You may be the next one needing assistance. Take time in the evenings to unwind and talk with volunteer friends about the events of the day. Discuss the incidents that brought tears or laughter. Pray for each other and for those you are helping. Tell your teammates how you see God working and the lessons He is teaching you.

Witnessing to Disaster Victims

There will be opportunity to witness on disaster projects, but acceptance of the gospel should not be linked to acceptance of assistance. Go to serve the people. When they ask, *Why are you here?*, explain that you want to share the love and blessings that God has given you.

At times God may direct you to boldly explain the plan of salvation; other times, an embrace might be the better witness. Be sensitive to God's leading, especially during this time when people are both angry with and open to God.

Be careful about giving simple answers to people who are in the midst of complex confusion and grief. Such answers are often given as an easy way out of really caring like Christ cared. Some examples of simple answers: "Everything will be all right." "At least you didn't lose your loved ones." "Everything works for good for those who love God." A better answer might be, "I cannot fully understand your loss and what has happened, but I want to try to bear it with you."

Rooftop Evangelism

Roger was driving through a neighborhood ravaged by Hurricane Andrew when he spotted a man working alone on a roof. In the heat and wind, the shirtless man was struggling to nail a roll of tar paper on the roof. It was not an uncommon scene.

One thing about the scene, however, struck Roger as unusual. The man on the roof had a red, raw scar that extended from his neck to his waist, and around to his back.

Stopping his truck, Roger said, "It looks like you need some help."

"Can't afford it," the man said. "Used my insurance money for materials."

"Doesn't matter," Roger said, climbing onto the roof. "See that truck. I'm with the Florida Baptist Convention, and we'd like to help you."

"I'm not a Baptist."

"I don't care what you are," Roger said as he held the roll so that it didn't slide. "Don't you want some help?"

The man paused and gave him a hard look.

Roger went on to say, "Seriously, we're just out here helping people. Couldn't you use some help?"

"I don't go to church."

"You're still not listening to me," Roger said. "I'll have a crew out here in the morning, and we'll help you finish this roof."

The next day the crew arrived and began work. Through the witness of team members, the man gave his life to Christ and is now an active member of a nearby Baptist church.

Effective mission volunteers do more than humanitarian works; they offer a life-giving faith in Christ through their actions and their words.

Session Seven
For Those with Home Mission Plans

Before You Go

1. Plan a cookout or get-together at someone's home. If all team members belong to one church, it is good to have a social event away from the familiar church setting. Focus on getting to know team members and their families.

2. If you do not have a team leader, appoint one. Also appoint someone to act as secretary to keep track of logistical preparations.

3. As a team, put together a list of items needed for the project you intend to do. Tools, VBS materials, medicine, audiovisual equipment, etc. Decide who will be responsible for which items. The secretary should keep a list.

4. Discuss transportation and accommodations. Decide who will drive and how much room you'll have for luggage and supplies. Decide who will pay fuel costs. Make a list of necessities and decide who will take items such as tents, camp stoves, grills, etc.

5. Discuss food. Will you be eating out, or will team members be providing and preparing food? If preparing your own meals, make a complete list of cooking and eating utensils and plan menus. Either have one person purchase needed food and all members help pay, or give each member a grocery list of items to take.

6. If you plan to do construction in a thinly populated area, either take all building supplies or have one member go ahead of the team to purchase supplies and have them on hand when the team arrives. In rural America, small-town hardware stores and lumberyards have been driven out of business by discount stores. You'll spend more time driving to a large town for supplies than you'll spend on a job site. Don't plan to buy any building materials at the site of a major disaster.

7. Discuss special abilities among team members that relate to the project. What do you feel comfortable doing or not doing? Work together as a team to make sure everyone has a job.

8. Discuss volunteers' particular talents that could be used in church services (singing, puppetry, drama, etc.).

9. Prepare a short testimony to be shared in church services.

10. If your team will be serving in several ways, have small group meetings. For example: block layers, cooks, crafts instructors, medical help. For each ministry or responsibility, make sure you have all the needed supplies and have worked out a plan of action. **Never go with the attitude,** We'll just find our way after we get there. Your best made plans may fall through, but at least have some plans.

11. Pray together as a team. Share burdens. Share joys. Tell of God's work in your life and be sure to share any Scripture verses that God has impressed on you.

On the Mission Tour

It is vital that the team meets together each day, preferably in the evening, to discuss the events of the day. In inner city and disaster situations, you will need to vent some of the emotional pressure. Especially in disaster areas you will be expected to keep up a cheerful front all the time, but the circumstances may be very depressing.

In rural areas (nondisaster-related) you may find yourself suppressing humor more than sorrow. A good time to share those hilarious one-liners that you choked back during the day is when you're together with the team. Always take time to share with each other the events that distressed you and the ones that amused you.

Be on the alert to help anyone on the team who is having trouble coping with a different culture. Help him understand that his feelings are normal. Above all, continually pray for one another.

When You Return Home

A week or so after your return, have a group meeting to evaluate the home mission experience. Discuss both positive and negative responses. (Refer to Debriefing Material at the end of chapter 22.)

You may encounter some cultural readjustment when you return. You will probably feel quite thankful for what you have. You may also feel angry about the waste and unthankful attitudes of those around you. These are normal feelings. It's a type of reverse culture shock. (Read Yo-yo Syndrome and Reverse Culture Shock in chapter 21.) Share your feelings with teammates who will understand your feelings; those who did not go on the mission trip will not understand.

You may be asked to give a presentation at your church. For tips on group presentations and individual ways to share your experiences, read chapter 22. In addition:

- Be very careful to not demean any racial, ethnic, or economic group.
- Avoid any judgmental statements.
- Don't present answers or solutions to the problems you witnessed other than Christ. There are no easy answers to a disaster or easy solutions for social ills.

Send a team thank-you note back to any special pastor or church leader who helped you on the project.

Epilogue

When one volunteer was asked why he went on so many mission trips, he said, "It's harder not to go than to go." *Prepared* volunteers usually have a good mission experience, and they volunteer again and again.

The ministry of volunteer mission service, however, is like other ministries: it carries a responsibility. As volunteers we are entrusted with the task of linking the home church to the mission field; we have a responsibility to improve that link.

As a fellow volunteer, I am still learning how to improve my volunteer service. Paul, the greatest of all cross-cultural missionaries, said, "Not that I have already obtained all this, or have already been made perfect, but I press on to take hold of that for which Christ Jesus took hold of me" (Phil. 3:12).

The long-term success of our ministry will depend on our ongoing commitment to logistical preparation, cross-cultural education, and spiritual development.

No matter how well we may perform on a specific tour, let us approach each new volunteer challenge with the attitude, "I know I can do this better," and then press on to improve our service.

Notes

Chapter 7: Spiritual Preparation
[1]Oswald Chambers, *My Utmost for His Highest* (Grand Rapids, MI: Discovery House Publishers, 1991), 187. Used by permission.
[2]Ibid., 187-188.

Chapter 13: Travel Day
[1]Dr. Karl Neumann, "Long Air Trips Can Be Less Tiring," *The Miami Herald,* March 21, 1993, 3F.

Chapter 16: Healthy Choices
[1]"Special Emphasis for Your Well-Being," *Crusade Manual* (Greenwood, IN: Men for Missions International), 23.

Chapter 19: In Search of a *Real* Missionary
[1]Some material for Forging Links and Mind Your Manners came from: "Your Visit to the Mission Field," *Christian Life* magazine (Chicago, IL: *Christian Life,* Strang Communications Co., June 1964).

Chapter 20: Love in Any Language
[1]Some material adapted from "Speaking Through an Interpreter," *Crusade Manual* (Greenwood, IN: Men for Missions International), 19-21; and "Suggestions to Those Who Speak Through an Interpreter," *Orientation Manual for Overseas Volunteers* (Richmond, VA: Foreign Mission Board of the Southern Baptist Convention, 1992), 38.
[2]Hannah Whitall Smith, *The Christian's Secret of a Happy Life* (Old Tappan, NJ: Fleming H. Revell Company, 1942), 138.

Chapter 23: Disaster Assistance
[1]"Safety Precautions and Instructions to All Volunteers," *Friends Disaster Service Handbook* (Peninsula, OH: Friends Disaster Service, 1989), 17.
[2]Ibid., 16.